Electronic
Magazines

Recent Titles in the
Praeger Series in Political Communication
Robert E. Denton, Jr., General Editor

Governmental Commission Communication
Edited by Christine M. Miller and Bruce C. McKinney

The Presidential Campaign Film: A Critical History
Joanne Morreale

High-Tech Campaigns: Computer Technology in Political Communication
Gary W. Selnow

Rhetorical Studies of National Political Debates: 1960–1992
Edited by Robert V. Friedenberg

Campaigns and Conscience: The Ethics of Politcal Journalism
Philip Seib

The White House Speaks: Presidential Leadership as Persuasion
Craig Allen Smith and Kathy B. Smith

Public Diplomacy and International Politics:
The Symbolic Constructs of Summits and International Radio News
Robert S. Fortner

The 1992 Presidential Campaign: A Communication Perspective
Edited by Robert E. Denton, Jr.

The 1992 Presidential Debates in Focus
Edited by Diana B. Carlin and Mitchell S. McKinney

Public Relations Inquiry as Rhetorical Criticism:
Case Studies of Corporate Discourse and Social Influence
Edited by William N. Elwood

Bits, Bytes, and Big Brother:
Federal Information Control in the Technological Age
Shannon E. Martin

Warriors' Words: A Consideration of Language and Leadership
Keith Spencer Felton

Electronic Magazines

Soft News Programs on Network Television

William C. Spragens

Praeger Series in Political Communication

Westport, Connecticut
London

Library of Congress Cataloging-in-Publication Data

Spragens, William C.
　　Electronic magazines : soft news programs on network television /
William C. Spragens.
　　　p. cm.—(Praeger series in political communication, ISSN
1062-5623)
　　Includes bibliographical references and index.
　　ISBN 0-275-94155-8 (alk. paper)
　　1. Television broadcasting of news—United States. 2. Documentary
television programs—United States. I. Title. II. Series.
PN4888.T4S73 1995
070.1'95—dc20　　94-42845

British Library Cataloguing in Publication Data is available.

Library of Congress Catalog Card Number: 94-42845
ISBN: 0-275-94155-8
ISSN: 1062-5623

First published in 1995

Praeger Publishers, 88 Post Road West, Westport, CT 06881
An imprint of Greenwood Publishing Group, Inc.

Printed in the United States of America

The paper used in this book complies with the
Permanent Paper Standard Issued by the National
Information Standards Organization (Z39.48-1984).

10　9　8　7　6　5　4　3　2　1

This book is dedicated to
Elaine J. Spragens,
survivor of many projects
and the author's best critic.

Contents

Series Foreword

Those of us from the discipline of communication studies have long believed that communication is prior to all other fields of inquiry. In several other forums I have argued that the essence of politics is "talk" or human interaction.[1] Such interaction may be formal or informal, verbal or nonverbal, public or private but it is always persuasive, forcing us consciously or subconsciously to interpret, to evaluate, and to act. Communication is the vehicle for human action.

From this perspective, it is not surprising that Aristotle recognized the natural kinship of politics and communication in his writings *Politics* and *Rhetoric*. In the former, he establishes that humans are "political beings [who] alone of the animals [are] furnished with the faculty of language."[2] And in the latter, he begins his systematic analysis of discourse by proclaiming that "rhetorical study, in its strict sense, is concerned with the modes of persuasion."[3] Thus, it was recognized over 2,300 years ago that politics and communication go hand in hand because they are essential parts of human nature.

Back in 1981, Dan Nimmo and Keith Sanders proclaimed that political communication was an emerging field.[4] Although its origin, as noted, dates back centuries, a "self-consciously cross-disciplinary" focus began in the late 1950s. Thousands of books and articles later, colleges and universities offer a variety of graduate and undergraduate coursework in the area in such diverse departments as communication, mass communication, journalism, political science, and sociology.[5] In Nimmo and Sanders' early assessment, the "key areas of inquiry" included rhetorical analysis, propaganda analysis, attitude change studies, voting studies, government and the news media, function and systems analyses, technological changes, media technologies, campaign techniques, and research techniques.[6] In a survey of the state of the field in 1983, the same authors and Lynda Kaid found additional, more specific areas of concern such as the presidency, political polls, public opinion, debates, and advertising to name a few.[7] Since the first study, they also noted a shift away from the rather strict behavioral approach.

A decade later, Dan Nimmo and David Swanson argued that "political communication has developed some identity as a more or less distinct domain of scholarly work."[8] The scope and concerns of the area have further expanded to include critical theories and cultural studies. While there is no precise definition, method, or disciplinary home of the area of inquiry, its primary domain is the role, processes, and effects of communication within the context of politics broadly defined.

In 1985, the editors of *Political Communication Yearbook: 1984* noted that "more things are happening in the study, teaching, and practice of political communication than can be captured within the space limitations of the relatively few publications available."[9] In addition, they argued that the backgrounds of "those involved in the field [are] so varied and pluralist in outlook and approach, . . . it [is] a mistake to adhere slavishly to any set format in shaping the content."[10] And more recently, Nimmo and Swanson called for "ways of overcoming the unhappy consequences of fragmentation within a framework that respects, encourages, and benefits from diverse scholarly commitments, agendas, and approaches."[11]

In agreement with these assessments of the area and with gentle encouragement, Praeger established the Praeger Series in Political Communication. The series is open to all qualitative and quantitative methodologies as well as contemporary and historical studies. The key to characterizing the studies in the series is the focus on communication variables or activities within a political context or dimension. As of this writing, nearly forty volumes have been published and there are numerous impressive works forthcoming. Scholars from the disciplines of communication, history, journalism, political science, and sociology have participated in the series.

I am, without shame or modesty, a fan of the series. The joy of serving as its editor is in participating in the dialogue of the field of political communication and in reading the contributors' works. I invite you to join me.

Robert E. Denton, Jr.

NOTES

1. See Robert E. Denton, Jr., *The Symbolic Dimensions of the American Presidency* (Prospect Heights, Ill.: Waveland Press, 1982); Robert E. Denton, Jr., and Gary Woodward, *Political Communication in America* (New York: Praeger, 1985; 2nd ed., 1990); Robert E. Denton, Jr., and Dan Hahn, *Presidential Communication* (New York: Praeger, 1986); and Robert E. Denton, Jr., *The Primetime Presidency of Ronald Reagan* (New York: Praeger, 1988).

2. Aristotle, *The Politics of Aristotle*, trans. Ernest Barker (New York: Oxford University Press, 1970), p. 5.

3. Aristotle, *Rhetoric*, trans. Rhys Roberts (New York: The Modern Library, 1954), p. 22.

4. Dan Nimmo and Keith Sanders, "Introduction: The Emergence of Political Communication as a Field," in *Handbook of Political Communication*, ed. Dan Nimmo and Keith Sanders (Beverly Hills, Calif.: Sage, 1981), pp. 11–36.

5. Ibid., p. 15.

6. Ibid., pp. 17–27.

7. Keith Sanders, Lynda Kaid, and Dan Nimmo, eds., *Political Communication Yearbook: 1984* (Carbondale: Southern Illinois University Press, 1985), pp. 283–308.

8. Dan Nimmo and David Swanson, "The Field of Political Communication: Beyond the Voter Persuasion Paradigm," in *New Directions in Political Communication*, ed. David Swanson and Dan Nimmo (Beverly Hills, Calif.: Sage, 1990), p. 8.

9. Sanders, Kaid, and Nimmo, *Political Communication Yearbook: 1984*, p. xiv.

10. Ibid.

11. Nimmo and Swanson, "The Field of Political Communication," p. 11.

Preface
and Acknowledgments

It became clear that one gap in the literature about broadcast programming could be found in the lack of serious studies about the mushrooming phenomenon of magazine programs on the three original commercial networks.

The author began this study with the hope of covering content on all three networks. It was determined, however, that tri-network analysis had to be limited to analysis of ratings because the subject matter kept growing.

Nevertheless, the historic CBS programming beginning with "60 Minutes" and continuing with "48 Hours," "West 57th" and "Street Stories" has been examined in some detail. Brief looks have been taken at "20/20" and "PrimeTime Live" on ABC. A definitive study remains to be done on these as well as "Day One" and "Turning Point." Further work also needs to be done on developing CBS programming such as "Eye to Eye with Connie Chung" as well as NBC's "Now with Tom and Katie" and "Dateline NBC."

It was also fortuitous that with the cooperation of such network executives as Roone Arledge, Howard Stringer and Eric Ober, it was possible to obtain brief interviews with Alan Wurtzel, ABC senior vice president for magazines and long-form programming, and Andrew Heyward, former executive producer of "Eye to Eye with Connie Chung" and "48 Hours," now executive producer of "The CBS Evening News," who gave details of the philosophy of CBS in delving into sociological backgrounds of current societal trends.

The cooperation of all individuals involved, including Carolyn S. Willis and Anita Kay Darnes, who worked, respectively, on the Bibliography and the tedious task of making the audio/video transcriptions used in addition to those developed by transcription services such as Burrelle's Transcripts and Journal Graphics, is much appreciated.

I am also indebted to Ralph M. Goldman of the Catholic University of America, who commented on the manuscript while it was in preparation, and to those who suggested various ideas during the gestation of this book.

Also my wife, Elaine J. Spragens, is owed a debt of appreciation for the disruption of daily schedules and all other inconveniences that go along with the writing of a book.

Finally I am indebted to Professor Robert E. Denton, Jr., of Virginia Polytechnic Institute and State University in Blacksburg, and to my editors at Praeger for their role in the conception, refinement of ideas and production of this book.

Electronic Magazines

Chapter One

The Development of
Magazine Programming

This analysis seeks to show the development of magazine programming on network television, tracing the origins of the original "60
Minutes" program to the situation in the mid-1990s in which each
major network has several such programs and most of them tend
to be well rated, especially the more established ones.

Our entire culture has felt the impact of television on the American
public. Numerous authors and analysts have noted its considerable
impact on the political system.[1]

Studies in the voluminous literature have examined entertainment
on television, and other works have analyzed facets of broadcast
news and feature coverage. But this book will focus on the evolution
of broadcast news/feature coverage from the original long-form
documentary, through documentary facets of early television
(influenced by print patterns) during the 1948–1969 period, to
modern personality-based programming, particularly since 1969.

We suggest a pattern may be found across the media. This
pattern finds feature coverage has evolved from the newspaper
rotogravure section of the 1920s and 1930s (along with motion
picture newsreels) and the early heyday of magazines (1900–1945)
into the broadcast programming of the past several decades. In the
1990s this broadcast coverage is packaged in both conventional
television programming and that of cable.

The documentary, a staple of background reporting in network television's early days (especially "sustaining" unsponsored

programming), has survived into the modern era in the form of public television programs and series. This educational programming tends to have a somewhat more elite audience.

Early documentaries were long-form programming filling an hour or ninety minutes of the evening prime period (even on occasion a two-hour or three-hour slot). Such analytic programs were inserted in the prime-time programming as "specials" (i.e., one-time airings).

Topics of "specials" were exemplified by Edward R. Murrow's "Harvest of Shame" on "CBS Reports," an exposé of the conditions in migrant labor camps in Florida, and by two other Murrow CBS programs—one dealing with "Automation" on Murrow/ Friendly's "See It Now" and the other dealing with the hydrogen bomb in the same series (an outgrowth itself of radio and recordings under the title "I Can Hear It Now," released on records in a three-part series). On the automation documentary, UAW president Walter Reuther and IBM president Thomas J. Watson, Jr., were interviewed, as well as a Ford Motor Company vice president and union bakery workers in Philadelphia.[2]

NBC carried "Omnibus" as a weekend broadcast that featured the coast-to-coast capability of early television network broadcasts (cumbersome equipment was used for this novelty of that day). "Omnibus" was contemporaneous with "See It Now" in the mid-1950s. According to Reuven Frank of NBC, this series alternated with another, known as "Kaleidoscope."[3]

Viewers able to recall the 1950s remember other examples of Edward R. Murrow's "See It Now," particularly the March 1954 broadcast in which Murrow presented his controversial coverage of the late U.S. Senator Joseph R. McCarthy (R-Wisconsin).[4]

Standard documentaries like this continued into the 1960s and occasionally into the 1970s and are still to be found today on the Public Broadcasting Service (PBS), overlapping the early development of electronic magazines on the traditional "Big Three" networks, ABC, CBS and NBC. An *electronic magazine program* is defined as a feature and personality-based television segment more oriented to the superficial or short-term viewer than one heavy on analysis and abstract concepts.

Electronic magazines' contents are extremely congenial to the television format. They draw larger audiences with mass appeal, in contrast to programming frequently found on cable networks or PBS.

Titles of the early-era documentary series included "CBS Reports," "NBC White Paper" and "ABC Special Report." In their traditional format (sometimes accompanied by a kind of "voice of doom" or authoritative narration like that of Westbrook van Voorhees on "The March of Time"), they dealt with foreign policy analyses or social problems or even public policy matters. An example is the "NBC White Paper" aired in the late 1960s; this was one of the first network broadcasts to carry revisionist views of President Kennedy's policy in South Vietnam.

Controversy surrounded some productions. One was the "CBS Reports" program "Harvest of Shame," already mentioned, which triggered a reaction from both the public and Congress. Advertiser response was negative as well, at least in some cases. In 1961 another in the "CBS Reports" series dealt with hunger in Mississippi and also attracted political controversy. Both were produced just before Murrow left CBS to become President Kennedy's director of the U.S. Information Agency (which embraced the Voice of America, then active as a principal resource in Cold War–era diplomacy).

The public opinion firestorm over the 1954 Murrow "See It Now" broadcast about Senator Joseph McCarthy could be explained in two ways. First, not only CBS but also the other two networks of the time had a long tradition of seeking to employ objectivity in journalism. Their attempt to deliver balanced views on controversial topics was not entirely voluntary but was an effort to comply with the provisions of Section 315 of the Communications Act of 1934. The act called for airing of different viewpoints on the public's airwaves; the administratively imposed FCC regulation required that "equal time" be given to opposing points of view or indeed an array of more than two viewpoints. The theory, as explained in Ithiel de Sola Pool's analysis of communications policy, was that the airwaves belonged to the public and therefore government should ensure that private sector broadcasters give access to a wide variety of opinions.[5]

The underlying assumption of Section 315 was that any public issue inherently has "opposing points of view." The term "opposing" leads to at least two possibly dubious conclusions: (a) equal time is given to unequal distributions of opinion; (b) cases where there are many points of view are reduced to two. Sometimes the consequences may be almost as distorting as the totalitarian emphasis on a single official viewpoint.

Murrow's view of Senator McCarthy (despite its resting on film clips showing McCarthy himself in action) was so edited as to present an unfavorable view of the Wisconsin senator. This editing itself brought down the wrath of conservative and right-wing commentators. This foreshadowed a pattern of conservative criticism of the media echoed in the editorial line of William Buckley's *National Review* as well as the 1993 view of President Clinton's controversial policy on military discipline (don't ask; don't tell), in which some of the public attacked both Clinton and the news media for what these individuals viewed as "furthering homosexuality" in Pentagon operations and indeed in the entire military establishment. Their views found an entertaining echo in the radio and videotape work, as well as in the books of commentator Rush Limbaugh.

Second, in the 1950s Senator McCarthy had spawned a reactionary climate of opinion (alarmist as well, a "Red scare" of proportions comparable to those of Attorney General A. Mitchell Palmer's anti-Communist witch hunt of 1920). McCarthy sought to capitalize on xenophobic American resentment of Marshal Josef Stalin and his early Cold War successors. McCarthy charged that varying numbers of Communists had infiltrated the Department of State. The American public of that day found this somewhat credible, after the conviction of Alger Hiss on perjury charges growing out of allegations by former *Time* editor Whittaker Chambers that Hiss engaged in espionage for the Soviet Union in the 1930s.[6]

Samuel Stouffer's research on communism, conformity and civil rights found that only about 3 percent of his national sample believed that communism was a real threat. This is a good example of the kinds of distortion created by, and then condemned by, the news media.[7]

Network objectivity rules under the Communications Act of 1934 required that the Federal Communications Commission (FCC) must enforce a public service requirement for licensing, under which varying viewpoints had to be represented as proof of the station's dedication to the public interest, convenience or necessity (language of the legislation). This initially applied to radio but was also found to relate to television when the FCC began dealing with this new medium. This federal licensing law and regulations growing out of it explain in part the CBS decision to offer Senator McCarthy "equal time" for reply after the damaging Murrow broadcast. In the end, McCarthy may have destroyed himself by overreaching;

his attacks led the Eisenhower administration to cooperate in the Army-McCarthy hearings of 1954, which ultimately led to McCarthy's downfall in the form of censure by the United States Senate a few months later.

Despite Murrow's success in focusing public opinion on McCarthy's abuses of the investigative power of Congress, there was also indirect censorship of network broadcasting. During the McCarthy scare, an organization called "Red Channels" published a newsletter using tactics of guilt by association. The newsletter "fingered" supposed offenders and subversives indiscriminately when they were suspected of the least taint of Communist, Communist-front, fellow traveling or left-wing connections. In the 1930s the Depression caused many citizens to engage in advocacy of socialist positions, which by the late 1940s had come to be interpreted as pro-Soviet. And by the 1950s the political climate had practically completed a 180-degree turn. One newscaster fired by CBS during this "guilt by association" or witch hunt period was the late William L. Shirer, who broadcast from Berlin during the 1930s and while in Berlin developed a strong anti-Nazi bias.[8] With a popular position during World War II, leftist organizations made people like Shirer vulnerable to attack during this time of hysteria. "Pro-Communist" charges were also leveled against nuclear scientist Dr. J. Robert Oppenheimer because of associations with his brother, a known leftist, and Haakon Chevalier, a French Communist. Although Oppenheimer had been hailed as a hero after taking a leading role in the World War II Manhattan Project for developing the atomic bomb, in the 1950s his security clearance was taken away at a hearing of a federal board.[9]

When Edward R. Murrow was attacked for the hunger program and "Harvest of Shame" at congressional hearings, other journalists and notables were criticized as well.[10]

In this opinion climate, CBS terminated William L. Shirer. He commented, "My ouster, I believe, marked the beginning of a new CBS policy of knuckling under to what it thought was the temper of the times. That Murrow would go along with it saddened me."[11]

With the increasing commercialization and ratings consciousness which occurred after the advent of television, "See It Now" finally lost its Alcoa sponsorship and gave way to "Person to Person," an apparent forerunner of such modern celebrity interview shows as "Entertainment Tonight" on syndicated release and the "Barbara Walters Specials" on ABC. "Person to Person" was perhaps the last series Murrow developed for CBS. Interviews were often conducted in celebrities' homes (both political and other celebrities were featured). "Person to Person" was broadcast with clumsy equipment, long before the minicam became popular even with the public, let alone commercial broadcasters. This genre of programming made lighter viewing and more superficial programming than documentaries, which traditionally carry low ratings and draw a relatively elite audience. This advent of personality-based series also drew the fire of critics of television, who saw the trend as an encroachment of commercialism on the public service aspects of broadcasting. Newton Minow, President Kennedy's chairman of the Federal Communications Commission, referred to the television programming of this era as a "vast wasteland."

In the "Person to Person" program with Senator and Mrs. John F. Kennedy, Jacqueline Kennedy in the 1950s spoke of a favorite poem of her husband, Rupert Brooke's "I Have a Rendezvous with Death," which JFK viewed as poignant and haunting.[12]

But perhaps a truer forerunner of the Barbara Walters ABC celebrity interviews may be found in a Murrow "Person to Person" aired April 9, 1954, and rebroadcast January 3, 1958, of an interview with two of the Marx Brothers comedy team, now made available on videotapes recorded from earlier kinescopes.[13]

Murrow closed out his active broadcast career in 1961, leaving CBS to take the Kennedy appointment at USIA. By that time he had poor health (he was a chain smoker) and he declined President Johnson's request to remain with the USIA. He died April 27, 1965.[14]

Shirer's comments about CBS indicate that the onetime Berlin correspondent felt that Murrow, on leaving CBS, was given the same treatment as he. Shirer cited Murrow's speech to broadcasters in which Murrow lectured the industry. (Similar views were expressed by anchor Dan Rather in 1993.)

A William S. Paley biographer, Lewis J. Paper, gives a different perspective of CBS management's reaction to the McCarthy broadcast controversy: "The CBS chairman said the company would provide him (Murrow) with bodyguards (after the McCarthy program). Murrow rejected this suggestion out of hand, but Paley would not be turned aside—he arranged for the protection without Murrow's knowledge." Paper also noted that President Eisenhower criticized Paley for permitting McCarthy to respond under the right of reply rules.[15]

The conflict between the commercial and informational sides of broadcast, perhaps intensified today with the advent of multi-channel cable (and even 500-channel cable in prospect) and intense competition for audiences, has a long history.[16]

Susan J. Douglas discussed this problem in analyzing the radio era of broadcasting: "[The] illusion of power residing with the audience rather than broadcasters was perpetuated in countless articles in the 1920s and emerged out of the journalistic conventions that cast radio as an agent of altruism."[17] There are valid comparisons of this view of broadcasting's role as a public opinion catalyst which parallels the use of talk shows as candidate outlets to voters in the 1992 Clinton-Bush-Perot presidential campaign.

Douglas Kellner viewed the networks as an establishment institution for corporate America and criticized them from a radical perspective, in contrast to the conservatives' criticism that the broadcasters do not conform to their ideology.[18] Kellner of course did not envision the irony of the 1992 talk show phenomenon and how it opened up avenues for Clinton and Perot which made Bush's tactics appear stale, antiquated and out of style, even allowing for the constraints put on him as an incumbent President.

More recently the networks appeared especially vulnerable to criticism from the left, whereas in a financial sense in the 1980s they were targets for potential successors to McCarthy such as Senator Jesse Helms (R-North Carolina) and Reed Irvine of Accuracy in Media, a conservatively sponsored analysis organization. Helms in 1985 called on corporate interests to aid a proposed takeover or buyout of CBS to "become Dan Rather's boss." Rather was denied Bush presidential interviews all during the 1989–1993 term of the forty-first President after the two men's confrontation in early 1988 and was only able to complete exclusive presidential interviews with the advent of President Bill Clinton during the Clinton inauguration week and the "48 Hours" special of that week in January 1993.

The foregoing leads to the conclusion that any meaningful analysis of television programming requires that the discussion be set in a context of media structure (Kellner, for example, notes striking differences between broadcast and print). Whatever action the media take, the previous discussion indicates that they will receive criticism all across the opinion spectrum.

Eric Alterman's 1991 interview with Bill Moyers, PBS analyst and former press secretary to President Lyndon B. Johnson, found Moyers echoing some of Kellner's criticism of the media. Moyers himself moved from print media (publisher of *Newsday*) to broadcast journalism, serving stints with CBS as a commentator before moving to his current work with PBS, specializing in documentaries much as the Cable News Network (CNN) specializes in rapid spot coverage.

Moyers admitted some culpability for the notorious "daisy" commercial in the 1964 presidential campaign, which depicted a small girl pulling petals off a daisy, followed by a nuclear mushroom cloud. It criticized Barry Goldwater's stance of letting military commanders in the field rather than the President decide on the use of nuclear weapons. The "daisy" commercial paralleled the 1991 "preemptive strike" commercials attacking Senators Joseph Biden (D-Delaware), Ted Kennedy (D-Massachusetts), and Alan Cranston (D-California) for allegedly sleazy behavior (plagiarism, Chappaquiddick, and the savings and loan debacle, respectively); however, Moyers blamed Vietnam, Watergate and the "national security mentality" for some of the corrosion of American values. Moyers added: "Even if everything the right says about liberals is true, it would still address only a small segment of the collapse of America's self-discipline."[19]

Moyers' prophetic and Calvinistic tone may reflect his training in the Edinburgh seminary as well as his service and his experiences in the broadcast industry.[20]

Analyzing the media industry's structure may be pointless unless its role is considered in relationship to other longstanding American institutions. For this purpose, a good case study of media-military relationships is available in earlier literature on this subject published shortly after the Persian Gulf crisis and war of 1990 and 1991.[21] The Gannett Foundation proposed these recommendations for reform as the result of its 1991 survey:

1. The American news media must learn to represent themselves collectively with one voice on matters of access to information and censorship in time of war without sacrificing the independence of individual media or their essential competitiveness. . . .

2. The news media must more effectively articulate the case for freedom of information in wartime than is understood by the general public. . . .

3. News organizations that covered the Gulf War need to assess carefully the qualifications and performance of their war correspondents with an eye toward future improvements.

4. ... [T]he pool system (collaborative reporting) should be used only as a temporary expedient, to be abandoned as soon as is consistent with genuine national security needs [determination of which needs are genuine will obviously be a point of military-media controversy].

5. The pool must also be reformed to include a mechanism for arbitrating judiciously between the needs of different media.[22]

The Gannett Foundation report, which also includes guidelines used for combat coverage, made general recommendations as well, including (in condensed form) use of diverse news sources by media to assure completeness and scope; information from media about how they cover combat; encouragement of public discussion and debate; acknowledgment of commitment of resources by major news outlets for combat coverage; journalism school focus on combat coverage in their curriculum; more attention in elementary and secondary schools to First Amendment freedoms.[23]

The media have a greater capacity to "package" background, "soft" news and feature material especially because of television's increasing diversity of channels in the age of dominant cable. But along with this increasing diversity has come a splintering of the audience. In the mass communications heyday (perhaps between 1965 and 1975) the network dominance was notable. But introduction of cable specialization of functions has transformed the context of information transmission. This has created problems for government, for journalists, for the computer and telecommunications industries, for public officials as well as other actors in government, and most of all for the public.

This study's thesis will be that the development of background-ers and "soft news" material, although deplored in some of the extreme forms as "tabloid journalism," has at least the potential for serving the public with balanced assessment of information as well as full facts. Further, we will trace the evolution of programming from early documentaries to the present-day array of prime-time magazine productions.

We shall turn next to the evolution of "soft news" in the electronic magazine format, the topic of Chapter Two.

NOTES

1. See Larry Sabato, *Feeding Frenzy: How Attack Journalism Has Transformed American Politics* (New York: Free Press, 1991); William C. Adams, ed., *Television Coverage of International Affairs* (Norwood, NJ: Ablex Publishing Corp., 1982); Frederic T. Smoller, *The Six O'Clock Presidency: A Theory of Presidential Press Relations in the Age of Television* (New York: Praeger, 1990); Jeffrey B. Abramson, P. Christopher Arterton and Garry R. Orren, *The Electronic Commonwealth* (New York: Basic Books, 1988); S. Robert Lichter, Stanley Rothman and Linda S. Lichter, *The Media Elite* (Bethesda, MD: Adler and Adler, 1986); Dan Nimmo and James E. Combs, *Mediated Political Realities*, second edition (New York: Longman, 1988); Charles Press and Kenneth VerBurg, *American Politics and Journalists* (Glenview, IL: Scott, Foresman, 1988); William C. Spragens, *The Presidency and the Mass Media in the Age of Television* (Lanham, MD: University Press of America, 1978); William C. Spragens, *From Spokesman to Press Secretary: White House Media Operations* (Lanham, MD: University Press of America, 1980); David Halberstam, *The Powers That Be* (New York: Random House, 1978); William E. Porter, *Assault on the Media: The Nixon Years* (Ann Arbor: University of Michigan Press, 1977); John R. MacArthur, *Second Front: Censorship and Propaganda in the Gulf War* (New York: Hill and Wang, 1992); Robert E. Denton, Jr., ed., *The Media and the Persian Gulf War* (Westport, CT: Praeger, 1993); Marcia Whicker, James Pfiffner and Raymond Moore, *The Presidency and the Persian Gulf War* (Westport, CT: Praeger, 1993); Martha J. Kumar, *Wired for Sound and Pictures: The President and White House Communications Policies* (Baltimore: Johns Hopkins University Press, forthcoming; Betty Houchin Winfield, *FDR and the News Media* (New York: Columbia University Press, 1985); Craig Allen Smith and Kathy B. Smith, *The White House Speaks: Presidential Leadership as Persuasion* (Westport, CT: Praeger, 1994); Bert E. Park, M.D., *Ailing, Aging, Addicted: Studies of Compromised Leadership* (Lexington: University Press of Kentucky, 1992); Matthew Robert Kerbel, *Edited for Television: CNN, ABC and the 1992 Presidential Campaign* (Boulder, CO: Westview Press, 1994); Philo C. Washburn, *Broadcasting Propaganda: International Radio Broadcasting and the Construction of Political Reality* (Westport, CT: Praeger, 1992); Conrad Smith, *Media and Apocalypse: News Coverage of the Yellowstone Forest Fires, Exxon Valdez Oil Spill, and Loma Prieta Earthquake* (Westport, CT: Greenwood Press, 1992).

2. "Harvest of Shame," CBS Reports, E. R. Murrow, airdate: Nov. 25, 1960 (available in Fox Video Set, Vol. 4, Edward R. Murrow, *Harvest of Shame*, narr. by Dan Rather, 1993); "Automation," E. R. Murrow, CBS, June 9, 1957 (available on Video Yesteryear, No. 241); "The Hydrogen Bomb," Studio 41, E. R. Murrow (packaged on video from CBS); Video, "See It Now Starring Edward R. Murrow" airdate not noted, (Goodtimes Golden TV Classics, copyright 1986). Also see *Goodnight and Good Luck, Vol. 2, The Best of See It Now* (Fox Video, CBS Reports Edited Selections, 1993).

3. Reuven Frank, *Out of Thin Air: The Brief Wonderful Life of Network News* (New York: Simon & Schuster, 1991).

4. This event is well covered in Joseph E. Persico, *Edward R. Murrow: An American Original* (New York: Dell Publishing, 1988), pp. 327–342. See also Alexander Kendrick, *Prime Time: The Life of Edward R. Murrow* (New York: Avon Books, 1969); Eric Sevareid, *Not So Wild a Dream* (New York: Random House, 1961).

5. Ithiel de Sola Pool, *Technologies of Freedom* (Cambridge, MA: Belknap Press, 1993).

6. This controversy continued in 1992 with disputes over the announcement by a member of the Yeltsin government in Russia that no documentation could be found of espionage by Hiss. See Alger Hiss, *In the Court of Public Opinion* (New York: Scribners, 1961); Whittaker Chambers, *Witness* (New York: Doubleday, 1959).

7. Samuel Stouffer et al., "Communism, Conformity and Civil Rights," *Public Administration Review* 16 (Winter 1956): pp. 40–52.

8. William L. Shirer, *20th Century Journey: The Nightmare Years, 1930–1940* (Boston: Little, Brown, 1984); Shirer, *20th Century Journey: A Native's Return, 1945–1948* (Boston: Little, Brown, 1990).

9. For background on J. Robert Oppenheimer, see McGeorge Bundy, *Danger and Survival: Choices About the Bomb in the First 50 Years* (New York: Random House, 1988); James W. Kunetza, *Oppenheimer: The Years of Risk* (Englewood Cliffs, NJ: Prentice-Hall, 1982); I. I. Rabi et al., *Oppenheimer: The Story of One of the Most Remarkable Personalities of the 20th Century* (New York: Charles Scribner's Sons, 1969); Philip M. Stern et al., *The Oppenheimer Case: Security on Trial* (New York: Harper & Row, 1969); entry for December 3, 1953, in Dwight D. Eisenhower, *The Eisenhower Diaries* (edited by Robert H. Ferrell) (New York: W. W. Norton & Co., 1981); Richard Pfau, *No Sacrifice Too Great: The Life of Lewis L. Strauss* (Charlottesville: University Press of Virginia, 1984); unpublished paper by author, "Security Clearances in the Eisenhower Era: The Case of Dr. J. Robert Oppenheimer," presented at Eisenhower Centennial Symposium, Gettysburg (PA) College, October 1990. Also see in video archives: Pyramid Home Video, *The Day After Trinity* (1981 video documentary by John Else); Peter Jennings, Vol. 2, *45/85: America and the World Since World War II* (covering McCarthyism and related phenomena), ABC News Video, 1985; *Fat Man and Little Boy: The Story of the Extraordinary People Who Changed Our World* (movie with Paul Newman dealing with the Oppenheimer role in the Manhattan Project, released by Paramount Pictures, 1989).

10. On criticism of Murrow and the background of the McCarthy era witch hunts, see Herbert Mitgang, *Dangerous Dossiers: Exposing the Secret War Against America's Greatest Authors* (New York: Donald I. Fine, 1988). This volume deals with subversion controversies from the Sacco-Vanzetti case in the 1920s through the Iran-Contra controversy which began in 1986. Files covered Pearl S. Buck, Theodore Dreiser, William Faulkner, Dashiell Hammett, Ernest Hemingway, Sinclair Lewis, Thomas Mann, John Dos Passos, Carl Sandburg, John Steinbeck, Thornton Wilder, Tennessee Williams and even Ambassador John Kenneth Galbraith, President Kennedy's ambassador to India. Also see Christopher Ogden, *Life of the Party: The Biography of Pamela Digby Churchill Hayward Harriman* (Boston: Little, Brown, 1994), pp. 158–183.

11. William L. Shirer, *20th Century Journey: A Native's Return, 1945–1948* (Boston: Little, Brown, 1990), p. 111.

12. Museum of Broadcasting audiotape, side two, band five, of *Walter Cronkite: Rare Voices of the 20th Century* (New York: Museum of Broadcasting, 1981), carries a segment of this "Person to Person" airing.

13. Edward R. Murrow, *Person to Person: Marx Brothers*, Video Yesteryear.

14. See Persico, *ibid*, and Kendrick, *ibid*.

15. Paley ironically defended the "fairness doctrine" to Eisenhower, a position rarely taken by broadcast management. Lewis J. Paper, *Empire: William S. Paley and the Making of CBS* (New York: St. Martin's Press, 1987), pp. 170, 171. See also Sally Bedell Smith, *In All His Glory: The Life of William S. Paley* (New York: Simon & Schuster, 1990).

16. See, for example, Larry Sabato, *op. cit.*; David Halberstam, *op. cit.*; David Halberstam, *The Best and the Brightest* (Greenwich, CT: Fawcett Crest Books, 1972); Fred W. Friendly, *Due to Circumstances Beyond Our Control* (New York: Vintage Books, 1968).

17. Susan J. Douglas, *Inventing American Broadcasting* (Baltimore: The Johns Hopkins University Press, 1987), p. 321.

18. Douglas Kellner, *Television and the Crisis of Democracy* (Boulder, CO: Westview Press, 1990), pp. 173, 174.

19. Eric Alterman, "Moyers on Washington," *Washington Post Magazine* 21, no. 2 (September 1, 1991), pp. 22, 23.

20. *Cablevision*, August 30, 1982, p. 18.

21. Gannett Foundation Media Center, *The Media at War: The Press and the Persian Gulf Conflict* (New York: Gannett Foundation/Freedom Forum, 1991), pp. 96, 97. See also Denton, *op. cit.*, pp. 27–42, and Whicker et al., *op. cit.*, pp. 153–175.

22. Gannett, p. 97.

23. Gannett, p. 97.

Early Soft News Programs: "60 Minutes"

"Soft news" may be defined as coverage which focuses on individuals, personalities and feature content more than "hard news," which is straight reporting of events.

"Soft news" programs were exhibited on networks as early as the Murrow "Person to Person" broadcasts. But the entity considered the original program of the modern "soft news" genre is the one-hour presentation "60 Minutes," begun by CBS News in 1968.

This chapter examines the development and evolution of the "60 Minutes" concept. Don Hewitt was the original producer. Mike Wallace as lead interviewer also developed "60 Minutes." Summaries of Wallace's program development with "Night Beat" and "Mike Wallace Interviews" will indicate how Wallace developed the role/function of the chief interviewer.

Broadcasting literature includes many analyses and memoirs about this network trailblazing hit. One is Wallace's own *Close Encounters*, originally published in 1984.[1] In 1980 Arno Press and CBS News jointly published *60 Minutes Verbatim*, based on stories aired during the 1979–80 season. Other program participants besides Wallace have contributed to the literature. Examples of their writings include Harry Reasoner's 1981 publication, *Before the Colors Fade*, and Morley Safer's *Flashbacks*, an account of his return visit to Vietnam, where he had served as a combat correspondent.[2]

Dan Rather, who participated in the program in the 1970s, published *I Remember*, but this volume was not directly related to his broadcasting career but rather described his early years and childhood.

Literature has appeared in the form of taped material sold commercially as well as in the traditional form of books. In 1984, CBS/Fox issued in Beta format a videotape entitled *The Best of 60 Minutes*. This was an anthology. Shirley Temple Black, then Ambassador of the United States to Ghana, was interviewed by Mike Wallace in one of the segments included in this tape. It also included a Harry Reasoner feature on "Mafia wars" in Palermo, an Ed Bradley story on male chauvinism in West Virginia coal mines, and an Andy Rooney satiric piece. Except for the last, all could be considered to have political content in the broader sense of the term. They also followed the "soft news" format in that the Ambassador was interviewed with more of a personality focus (people oriented), and the same was true of the Bradley story on abuses of women in the mining industry. The Mafia wars story by Reasoner not only followed the soft news format but also introduced a theme of crime coverage which has been a thread running all through the more than twenty-five years that "60 Minutes" has been broadcast.

In 1985, CBS/Fox issued a sequel video, *The Best of 60 Minutes, Volume Two*, sold in the VHS format. This production included a Dan Rather exposé on con artists promoting unneeded car repairs for unwary motorists; a Mike Wallace feature on deaf students at Washington, D.C.'s Gallaudet College; a Morley Safer piece on the type of retarded geniuses dealt with in the popular movie "Rain Man"; and a Harry Reasoner story on the use of drugs at the nation's racetracks. In categorizing these segments, the first and last appeared to deal with crime and thus could be termed political in terms of problems dealt with by the justice system. The retarded geniuses segment was more psychological than political. An Andy Rooney satire on television commercials dealing with pharmacies could be described as non-political in basic content.

The most recent serious study about "60 Minutes" focused on production techniques and was authored by Richard Campbell of the University of Michigan, *60 Minutes and the News: A Mythology for Middle America*, published in 1991.[3]

Other magazine shows such as "Street Stories," "Saturday Evening with Connie Chung," "Eye to Eye with Connie Chung," "Verdict" with Rita Braver on CBS; "20/20," "PrimeTime Live" and "Day One" on ABC; and numerous NBC efforts at soft news, including

"Now with Tom and Katie" and the controversial "Dateline NBC," will be analyzed in varying detail later in this study.

THE ORIGINS OF "60 MINUTES"

Mike Wallace started in radio in 1939, working at WOOD in Grand Rapids, Michigan, and WXYZ in Detroit. He also worked with Douglas Edwards, first anchor of CBS Evening News. In Chicago from 1941 to 1951 he worked on "The Air Edition of the *Chicago Sun*" with radio professional Clifton Utley. After leaving the Navy in 1956 Wallace worked on WGN, Chicago, in a radio interview show, "Famous Names." He later was on "The Chez Show" with Buff Cobb. In 1951 CBS invited the Wallace/Cobb team to New York to produce "Mike and Buff," another interview program. After working as a news anchor at Du Mont's Channel 5 in New York, Wallace began "Night Beat," also on Channel 5. Some consider this the probable forerunner to "60 Minutes." After other programs and a stint at KTLA-TV in Los Angeles, Wallace joined CBS, where he worked on both morning and evening news programs.[4]

At this time Don Hewitt, who produced evening news programs between 1948 and 1964, began producing documentaries.

Wallace wrote of Hewitt that he

discovered that—for him, at least—producing documentaries left much to be desired. . . . At some point in 1967, there began to evolve in Hewitt's mind an idea for a different kind of broadcast. If the "Evening News" was the television equivalent of a daily newspaper—the electronic front page, as it were—and a documentary was comparable to a nonfiction book that thoroughly examined one subject, then the program he envisioned could properly be described as a magazine. It would be a weekly or biweekly broadcast consisting of several stories on a wide range of topics—from politics to the arts, from interviews with world leaders to profiles of movie stars, from in-depth reports on the latest crisis at home or abroad to light features on scuba diving and health spas. Hewitt even came up with a title for the program. He wanted to call it "60 Minutes."[5]

Harry Reasoner was originally considered for the show, but when it went on the air, he and Mike Wallace appeared together. During 1968 the program was being put together and it was first broadcast on Tuesday, September 24, 1968, when the stopwatch that was to be the program's trademark was first seen on the television screen.

The opening program featured visits to the convention hotel rooms of Richard Nixon and Hubert Humphrey, an exclusive for CBS, at the time of their nominations for the presidency in 1968. Another feature was Mike Wallace's interview with Attorney General Ramsey Clark, termed the nation's "top cop." The final segment was an offbeat Sam Bass film entitled *Why Man Creates* (the film had been commissioned by Kaiser Aluminum).

During the program's first fall, interviews were completed with Hubert Humphrey and George Wallace, the governor of Alabama and an Independent presidential candidate. A Richard Nixon interview in October dealt with such matters as the Alger Hiss case and the 1960 campaign against John F. Kennedy. An early 1969 interview was with Vice President-elect Spiro T. Agnew, who resigned four and a half years later. Agnew was furious because Wallace reported on his mediocre high school grades, something which Wallace did not consider "character assassination."[6]

Other interviewees during 1969 were John and Martha Mitchell (the Nixon Attorney General and his wife); Black Panther leader Eldridge Cleaver; Coretta Scott King (widow of the Reverend Dr. Martin Luther King); Archbishop Fulton J. Sheen; and others.[7] In 1971 an interview was completed with former President Lyndon B. Johnson at the LBJ Ranch during the time of the opening of the Johnson Library in Austin, Texas. After having refused to discuss Vietnam, Johnson brought up the subject himself.

It was during this time that NBC tried its first program in the newsmagazine format, "First Tuesday."

Occasional contributions to "60 Minutes" were made by Eric Sevareid, Charles Collingwood, Robert Trout, Hughes Rudd and Heywood Hale Broun, none of whom was a permanent correspondent. Eventually the regulars on the program came to include Morley Safer, Dan Rather and Ed Bradley, as well as Mike Wallace.[8]

When Harry Reasoner went to ABC, Charles Kuralt (busy with "On the Road") did not want to join the "60 Minutes" staff, so Morley Safer became the new correspondent on the program. Although Mike Wallace came late to the Watergate story, according to Gary Paul Gates, he broadcast some tough interviews on the topic in 1973 and 1974. One of these was a June 1973 interview with Nixon domestic aide John Ehrlichman. Another Nixon administration figure, interviewed in 1970, was Interior Secretary Walter Hickel, later fired by Nixon. Not an administration figure, but an object of a highly controversial interview, was an ITT lobbyist, Dita

Beard. She had written a memo, discovered by Jack Anderson and Brit Hume, which indicated an "arrangement" between the Justice Department and ITT in which an antitrust case would be dropped and a $400,000 ITT contribution would be made to the 1972 Republican convention.[9]

Other interviews of that era were completed with Chuck Colson, the Watergate ex-convict and later head of the Prison Ministry; G. Gordon Liddy, another Watergate ex-convict; Nixon aide H. R. Haldeman; Eldridge Cleaver (object of a second interview while in exile in Paris in 1975); Clint Hill, the Secret Service agent who was in President Kennedy's Dallas motorcade; Maureen Reagan, daughter of Ronald Reagan and Jane Wyman; Governor Reagan (elected President in 1980); and former Treasury Secretary John B. Connally.[10]

In July 1980 Wallace interviewed Ronald and Nancy Reagan. Numerous interviews in the early years also dealt with Vietnam. On his earlier program Wallace had interviewed Madame Nhu (sister-in-law of South Vietnamese President Ngo Dinh Diem) in 1962; General William Westmoreland was another interviewee. In the pre–"60 Minutes" period Wallace also interviewed South Vietnam's later President, Nguyen Van Thieu. A controversial interview about the My Lai massacre included Seymour Hersh of the *New York Times* and a soldier named Paul Meadlo who had participated in "breaking" the My Lai story. Another interview regarding a PX scandal in Vietnam involved a conversation with Brigadier General Earl F. Cole. Wallace interviewed William J. Crum, whom Senate investigators had not been able to find, and the scandal resulted in General Cole's demotion to colonel and his early retirement, a result some of Cole's friends blamed on "slanted" reporting by Wallace and his colleagues.[11]

Another interview which eventually led to a legal controversy was done in fall 1971 with Lieutenant Colonel Anthony Herbert. In 1969 Herbert had been relieved of his command by Brigadier General John Barnes. After this action, Herbert accused General Barnes and Colonel J. Ross Ranklin, Barnes' deputy, of covering up war crimes and atrocities he had reported to them in Vietnam. The actual interview with Herbert was completed on January 23, 1973; in it Wallace confronted Herbert with the lack of substantiation of his story by other military sources. On February 4, 1973, "60 Minutes" carried a segment entitled "The Selling of Colonel Herbert," dealing with his charges. A sequel to this segment, aired on "CBS Reports" in 1982 under the title "The Uncounted Enemy: A Vietnam Deception," brought on an infamous lawsuit involving the network and General William Westmoreland. It ended out of court.[12]

In spring 1971 Wallace conducted an interview with Israeli General Moshe Dayan. Other Middle East leaders interviewed included Libyan strongman Moammar Qadaffi (Kadafhi), Syrian President Hafez Assad, PLO Leader Yasser Arafat, Israeli Prime Minister Menachem Begin, Egyptian President Anwar Sadat (assassinated in October 1981), and Shah Mohammed Reza Pahlavi of Iran. Still another interview was done with the Shah's successor, the Ayatollah Khomeini.[13]

In December 1975, "60 Minutes" was moved from 6 P.M. to 7 P.M. on CBS, placing it in early prime time. The Wallace-Gates account notes:

[B]y 1975 the program was well on its way to becoming a national institution, and the decision to move it back into prime time was yet another push in that direction. The switch occurred at a time when the CBS network was taking its lumps in the ratings. . . . [I]n the 1975–1976 season, a remarkable surge by ABC . . . enabled it to soar past both its rivals and relegate CBS to the unwonted misery of second place. Drastic afflictions call for drastic cures. So, more or less in desperation the alarmed and frustrated CBS programmers were willing to try anything that year; "60 Minutes" was ordered into the fray.[14]

At the request of Don Hewitt in 1975, Dan Rather joined the "60 Minutes" correspondent staff. According to Wallace:

[A] softer, less combative image worked entirely to Rather's advantage, and, as Wallace had predicted, it gave his career a big boost, leading ultimately to his being named to succeed Walter Cronkite as anchorman on the "CBS Evening News." . . .
Dan Rather was not the only beneficiary of that decision. Although Morley Safer's first reaction to "The Third Man Theme" was negative, it wasn't long before he came to regard Rather's presence on "60 Minutes" as an unexpected blessing. He had opposed bringing in a third correspondent because he didn't want to add to the heavy pressure he was already feeling from Wallace. . . . Because they were so similar in style and attitude, Wallace and Rather did spend a lot of time going after the same kind of hard-hitting, investigative stories, and in contrast, Safer's urbane features and ironic essays were seen in sharper relief. . . . Wallace and Rather brought considerable strengths to their work, but neither was in Safer's class as a stylist.[15]

Although Hewitt was instructed to condense program content for a time, later when the show became top-rated, network programmers sought to extend the prime-time schedule so the full show could be seen. So in spring 1978 Hewitt requested a fourth correspondent.[16]

Regarding the fourth correspondent, Ed Bradley (in 1993 the chief correspondent on "Street Stories"), Wallace and Gates noted that Bradley "had earned his stripes as a war correspondent in Vietnam" and covered the 1976 presidential campaign. He became the first African American CBS correspondent, and in 1978 Harry Reasoner returned from ABC to CBS, in time for the show's 10th anniversary.[17]

When Wallace and Gates wrote about "60 Minutes," Dan Rather had just left "60 Minutes" to become "CBS Evening News" anchor. During the latter part of Rather's time on "60 Minutes," the CBS News staff collaborated on a book-length anthology, *60 Minutes Verbatim*.[18] A few of the programs produced during the 1979–80 season and covered in this publication are commented on later.

Only segments with political subject matter have been analyzed, because of the nature of this volume. Other contents are briefly examined in Appendix I.

September 16, 1979, found a segment "On Trial for Murder" dealing with the court system; this had obvious political content in the term's broader sense. Harry Moses produced this Mike Wallace interview with an Orange County, California, gynecologist-obstetrician, Dr. William Waddill, who was on trial for murder after he had been hired to perform a legal abortion.

This segment was produced only six years after the major Texas case of *Roe v. Wade* was decided in the U.S. Supreme Court. In this litigation, Sarah Weddington's client won the right to have an abortion performed. Justice Harry A. Blackmun's ruling established a three-trimester formula for degrees of permissibility in abortions.

Noting the case's outcome, Wallace mentioned the eleven to one vote for Dr. Waddill's acquittal. Seeking to develop unbiased analysis of the explosive abortion issue, Wallace interviewed both Assistant District Attorney Bob Chatterton and defense attorney Charles Weedman. Wallace described the gynecological practice of Dr. Waddill in Orange County. Chatterton represented what came to be known as the "right to life" stance. The controversy arose because after the fetus was removed from the womb, it showed some signs of life on its own. The public expects impartial analysis of controversial issues of this type; when criticism of "60 Minutes" has arisen in lawsuits and elsewhere, it has been in instances where some of the public at least has viewed the coverage as biased, slanted or incomplete. (The Herbert case was discussed earlier.)

In producer Leslie Edwards' May 4, 1980, segment, "Palm Springs," interviews were done with two quite different clergymen, the Reverend Jesse Jackson and the Reverend Dr. Billy Graham. Questions centered on opposition by individual Jews to some traditional African American stances on civil rights. U.S. Supreme Court cases analyzed included three—those of Allan Bakke (so-called reverse discrimination in professional school admissions), De Funis, and Weber (both cases dealing with discrimination in employment practices).[19] Dan Rather sought Graham's and Jackson's views on whether such cases would promote fresh instances of anti-Semitism. Rather sought to divine causes of deterioration of cooperation between Jews and African Americans since the civil rights movement had peaked in 1965. Reverend Jackson noted the lack of "economic substance" in Black-Jewish relationships. The segment followed by a few days UN Ambassador Andrew Young's resignation from the Carter administration because of a controversy about informal contacts he had made with Palestinians (specifically the PLO). Since Rather's impartiality was challenged nine years later by no less than incumbent Vice President George Bush, the lack or presence of bias in this segment ought to be of interest in foreshadowing problems of that kind which Rather might have anticipated in the intervening years. At the time, Jackson was scheduled to meet soon with Yasser Arafat, the PLO leader. Both clergymen expressed interest in a Middle East settlement, but they spoke for widely divergent viewpoints. Rather's questions seemed to bring these differences into focus without appearing inflammatory.

Philip Scheffler, on September 23, 1979, produced a segment with Dan Rather, "Oil in the Bank," concerning the politics of oil in the Middle East—the subject of a Daniel Yergin book and the PBS series "The Prize" during the 1980s—which began with Rather's background discussion on the 1973 OPEC oil embargo which severely stressed Western nations' economies. How a series of American administrations worked to develop a strategic oil reserve was the core of the investigation. One interviewee, Tom Noel, who worked for both the Ford and Carter energy departments, felt excessive idealism in the Carter years complicated the task of building up the oil reserve. This piece seemed more informational than polemic.

On October 7, 1979, and again on May 18, 1980, Dan Rather and producer Jeanne Solomon dealt with "Who Killed Georgi Markov?" This case was believed to have been an espionage murder which occurred in London through the use of an umbrella armed with a poisoned dart. Victim Georgi Markov was a turncoat Bulgarian Communist writer who went into exile in the United Kingdom. Markov's British widow told Rather she did not know whether the stranger with the umbrella was a Bulgarian agent or "a friend trying to warn her husband."

Also interviewed by Rather was Dr. David Gall, the surgeon who removed the small pellet shot from the umbrella. A Scotland Yard investigation noted that Markov read news over Radio Free Europe (RFE). Cyril Panov, Markov's boss at RFE, noted that Markov's broadcasts had criticized Bulgarian Communists as a privileged class. Panov called the criticism "very mild." Rather then referred to previous KGB assassination plots against the West, which he said had been documented. Dr. Nikolai Kholkov, another interviewee, felt that the killing was to "send a message" rather than merely to eliminate Markov.

Rather's explication of the assassination theory was relatively detailed for television. It could hardly be expected that the KGB would have cooperated at that time with a Western correspondent's investigation, so the interview by its nature was one-sided. It was an attempt to explain a baffling uncertainty of motive, although the slaying's object would be guessed with some feeling of certainty.

CRIME AND LAW ENFORCEMENT COVERAGE

Barry Lando produced an October 14, 1979, segment on "The Stolen Cezannes," $3 million worth of paintings stolen from the Chicago Art Institute—a piece categorized under the heading of criminal justice. Museum director Laurence Chalmers was interviewed by Mike Wallace.

Barry Lando took a copy of a masterpiece to Canadian Customs in Montreal after a flight from New York; the agent asked him to wait while he conducted an Interpol check. No theft having been reported, Canadian Customs allowed Lando to proceed. Returning to New York, Lando was waved through by American Customs, no questions asked. Wallace's interview further probed into the workings of Interpol and various official agencies regarding art thefts. Wallace also asked Allan Maraynes, a "60 Minutes" researcher, to try to steal a genuine Utrillo work taken from the wall of a Wallace friend. A phony bill of sale was accepted by Sotheby Park Bernet and the item was to be put up for auction.

This kind of "reality check" is frequently used as a test by magazine programs. (Some magazine shows run into trouble as NBC's "Dateline NBC" did with a faked explosion which caused the threat of a General Motors lawsuit. Sometimes the object of the "test" complains about deceptive broadcast practices. Presumably abuses should be prevented through the application of the "CBS Standards," but the experience of NBC and its owner, GE, with the General Motors segment shows that even producers for networks and such broadcasters as Jane Pauley and Stone Phillips fall into traps sometimes with these efforts to get stories.

The resolution of the art theft came when a man posing as a friend of the thief was arrested by Chicago authorities; Wallace ended the segment thus. Other ruses which have been used in coverage include those involving hidden cameras, a favorite of ABC News, which used one in a "PrimeTime Live" segment dealing with accusations against Food Lion grocery chain that it was selling tainted meat or products that were not properly dated.

The customs inspection in this segment did not appear to abuse standards but producers and interviewers do sometimes get sloppy in applying standards. The dispute between ABC and Food Lion is still pending, but as a result of the GM truck story, NBC was obliged to issue an on-air apology to prevent a lawsuit by GM.

On October 21, 1979, Marion Goldin produced the segment "Edwin Rubin, M.D." about an investigation by the MediCal Fraud Unit of the California attorney general's office. Mike Wallace probed into the career of Dr. Rubin as an example of MediCal's inquiries. Dr. Joel Hendler was described as an eyewitness to alleged malpractice by Dr. Rubin. Wallace then pointed the finger at Senator Edward Kennedy (D-Massachusetts), who refused to discuss the congressional investigation of MediCal. Governor Jerry Brown refused to appear. Were Kennedy and Brown put off by Wallace's "gotcha" method of interviewing or was there some undisclosed information about these cases? Wallace raised questions but left the matter hanging as of that date. Was this suited to CBS guidelines?

Later, in a program on December 9, 1979, Wallace read a letter from Senator Kennedy to his constituents saying pertinent data about the MediCal investigation had been turned over to the Justice Department. Wallace said Kennedy also disputed Wallace's refusal to interview the staff director of Kennedy's health committee. Apparently there was a standoff when Wallace felt it was beneath his dignity to interview a Senate staff director.

In these and other segments aired at that time, balance seemed to be provided when all parties were interviewed and the format was more that of a feature story rather than a hard-digging exposé (although "60 Minutes" is known for these). A useful question for analyzing controversial broadcast segments such as the MediCal story is, How would other news organizations like the *New York Times*, NBC News, CNN, PBS and ABC News have handled the topic? We can speculate on what we know about the policies of these news organizations. One of the most responsible kinds of coverage would have been that of MacNeil-Lehrer, and CNN would have had a somewhat more Establishment or conservative orientation than the broadcast networks (whether that is related to the positions of the owners of national cable systems will not be discussed here, but it is known that Ted Turner of CNN and TBS believes network programs are too confrontational). Would NBC have handled the matter as it did the GM coverage, or would ABC have been more sensational, as with Food Lion? The exposé methods used by Wallace have spread so that it is doubtful that there was a high degree of difference in the approaches of the broadcast or even cable networks in 1994. But perhaps a divergence may occur.

GREAT DEPRESSION AND SUPREME COURT

Steve Glauber produced a November 4, 1979, segment with Dan Rather narrating the inscription on the State of Liberty, "Give Me Your Tired, . . ." It dealt with illegal immigrants (a news topic during the time of the Zoe Baird and Kimba Wood would-be appointments for Attorney General by President Clinton in 1993). Rather's interviewees included an unidentified immigration official, Immigration and Naturalization Service (INS) agent Ralph Raimond, California official Joe Razo, garment workers, employers, California clothing industry spokesman Bernard Brown, and

clothing manufacturer Jody Toteek Company's board chairman
Jack Weingarten, as well as ILGWU agent Max Wold. The Rather
piece was not advocacy journalism as much as an effort to enlighten
the public regarding the problem of undocumented aliens. Later,
in the Reagan era, there would be much discussion of Nicaraguan
refugees and the Sanctuary movement, but in 1979 all that lay in
the future.

A figure who was to play a major role in the 1980s was introduced
to the "60 Minutes" audience on November 18, 1979, when Barry
Lando produced a segment, "The Ayatollah," which included Mike
Wallace's interview with Ayatollah Khomeini. The encounter was
in the Moslem holy city of Qum. The religious leader stressed the
people of Iran's desire for the return and prosecution of Shah
Mohammed Reza Pahlevi. Khomeini also repeated charges of spying and said President Jimmy Carter could have all the Embassy
hostages released by sending the Shah back (implying a likely
conviction and execution). This story ended with a note by Dan
Rather describing a news conference three American hostages were
allowed to give. This story was being so widely covered in all media
and nationalistic passions on both sides were so inflamed at the
time that it was not difficult to hear different versions of the story
than that of the Ayatollah.

What degree of public exposure should the U.S. Supreme Court
justices sustain? This question arose in a segment, "The Brethren,"
aired December 2, 1979, which included an interview by Mike Wallace
with Bob Woodward, who with Scott Armstrong, a *Washington Post*
colleague, had coauthored an examination of *The Brethren* on the
Court. Wallace described it as "painstaking, carefully researched
and therefore explosive." One question dealt with the skills of Chief
Justice Warren Burger, about whom Woodward said Associate
Justice Lewis Powell had worries.

Woodward denied that any documents he used in writing the
book were stolen and said everyone questioned had legal access to
information. Obviously, the mystique of the Court was at stake and
many in the legal profession had objections to both the book and
the televised interview.

Woodward had been in a similar controversy over his book *Veil*,
which dealt with the career of director of central intelligence (DCI)
William Casey during the Reagan administration. Casey's family
denied that Woodward could have been admitted to Georgetown

University Hospital, where the controversial intelligence chief lay dying.

ENVIRONMENT, OPEC AND CONNALLY

Mike Wallace on December 16, 1979, applied the label of "corporate outlaw" to the Hooker Chemical Corporation. It was in a segment produced by Harry Moses entitled "The Hooker Memos," which told the story of the Love Canal environmental disaster area near Buffalo, New York, in the Niagara Falls area.

Cited by Wallace were pledges by Hooker to clean up an environmentally damaged lake in Michigan ($15 million at stake) and to pay for damages from toxic pesticide waste at Hooker's Occidental Chemical plant at Lathrop, California.

Wallace examined memos written by Robert Edson, environmental engineer for Hooker at the Lathrop plant. Edson would not appear on camera, but Wallace said he didn't need to. Wallace did interview Hooker president Don Bader, who asked Wallace to read a statement of appreciation for the Hooker cleanup from Charles Carnahan, executive officer of the California Regional Water Quality Control Board.

In this case, Wallace presented the claims against Hooker and the Hooker president took advantage of the opportunity to reply. Interviewed on the program was Tennessee Congressman Albert Gore, Jr. (later a Senator and in 1993 Vice President and author of an environmental best-seller, *Earth in the Balance*), who said the cleanup problem was industrywide. Wallace closed by noting that California Attorney General George Deukmejian (Governor Pete Wilson's predecessor as Governor) planned to file an environmental lawsuit against Hooker.

Don Hewitt produced a major segment, "The Sheik," on December 23, 1979, on which both Harry Reasoner and Mike Wallace presented material on the man who then spoke for OPEC (later fired by the Saudi royalty), Sheikh Ahmed Zaki Al-Yamani. They discussed the Arabian oil industry and the sheik noted that his country was the only one that "did not kick you out." This was a straight interview with the correspondents introducing only background material. Some discussion followed about Yasser Arafat.

Former Texas Governor John Connally, Treasury secretary under Richard M. Nixon, was the December 30, 1979, interviewee in the segment "Big John" produced by Philip Scheffler. Connally was asked about his conversion to the Republican party. (As Democratic governor of Texas, he was with President John F. Kennedy the day JFK was assassinated in November 1963 in Dallas and Connally was himself wounded.)

Connally was asked his views on Middle East oil and a controversial statement he had made about the Reverend Dr. Martin Luther King when King was assassinated: "Those who live by the sword die by the sword." Congresswoman Barbara Jordan was quoted as saying she was distressed by this remark. Connally also denied saying that "more people died at Chappaquiddick" than at Three Mile Island (scene of a 1970s environmental disaster). The segment gave a somewhat negative assessment of Connally, although the former Cabinet officer said he was improving his standing in the polls. (He briefly ran for the Republican presidential nomination in 1980 before Governor Ronald Reagan was nominated.)

"Roy Cohn," the subject of the final 1979 segment, was dealt with in the Joe Wehrshba–produced segment narrated by Morley Safer. The segment dealt with Cohn's background with Senator Joseph McCarthy in the 1950s. Benson Ford, suing his uncle, Henry Ford II, for scores of millions, was one client of Cohn's interviewed by Safer. Ken Auletta, author of media critical study *Three Blind Mice*, was also interviewed on Cohn's legal career. Dan Rather concluded the segment by declaring that Roy Cohn "was determined to get rich, and he has." The tone of the piece was not totally negative, but it was hardly an encomium.

One letter quoted for that evening was from Dr. Henry A. Kissinger, who objected to a statement about his views on Micronesia. Rather said the statement Kissinger objected to was given to CBS by former Nixon Interior Secretary Walter Hickel of Alaska.

REAGAN, KENNAN, THE IRS AND SOVIET TV

On January 6, 1980, William K. McClure produced the segment "CCCP-TV in Moscow" with Harry Reasoner as correspondent. Programming emanating from the TV tower in Moscow in the Brezhnev era of the old Soviet Union was analyzed. Reasoner noted, "From the standpoint of what a Communist government wants to do with its population, television might have been invented for the rulers of today's Soviet Union."

Reasoner spoke with Soviet television figures such as Henrikus

Jushkevitshus and Volodya Posner. He closed with the observation that "last Wednesday, 'Vremya,' that major nightly news program, used two domestic stories before getting around to reading the Tass story about Afghanistan, without pictures."

The element was chiefly informational, but it is hard to imagine a 1980 segment about the Soviet Union that would have provided a neutral viewpoint at that stage of the Cold War.

The print and electronic media in 1988 were full of stories about a confrontation between Dan Rather and then–Vice President George Bush, the heir apparent to the Republican presidential nomination that year. But in 1980 Rather conducted a less confrontational interview under the title "George Who?" produced by Joel Bernstein. Bush was then the leading challenger against Ronald Reagan for the 1980 Republican nomination. Before Rather read Bush a quotation from John Connally, Bush (even then with a chip on his shoulder) told Rather, "Clean it up now when you say anything." Rather asked Bush ironically about a *Christian Science Monitor* story which asked whether Bush was "too nice to be president." Rather said, "there are people out there who say George Bush is a nice fellow but he's all hat and no cattle. Which is to say he has no base." Bush talked about erosion in Reagan's public opinion position, then later in 1980 became Reagan's running mate. There was a bit of friction in the interview but it was nothing like the explosive one eight years later. Bob Schieffer of CBS said when Bush let Rather have it in 1988, Roger Ailes held up a sign in front of Bush reading "NOW!"[20] So Bush then talked about Rather's shortcomings and Rather did not get Bush to admit he had any improper dealings with Manuel Noriega of Panama. The 1980 segment ended with a speaker who compared George Bush to "the American eagle." It was hardly a real tipoff to the fireworks later in the decade.

Morley Safer summarized January 20 mail which included letters praising the Bush interview or saying it was "clumsy."

Dan Rather interviewed Ronald Reagan, former Governor of California, on the segment "The Frontrunner?" produced by Joel Bernstein for "60 Minutes" January 27, 1980. Rather asked about Reagan's decision regarding the Iowa caucuses, where Reagan did not campaign. Reagan said it might be possible to institute a blockade of Cuba but otherwise was cautious in his remarks. Reagan also denied his foreign policy experience was slim to none, citing a meeting he had had with Chiang Kai-shek as well as another with Leonid Brezhnev. Reagan also denied his age was a problem and the interview ended there. Reagan could have said that Rather "didn't lay a glove on him." But some current questions were raised.

February 10, 1980, brought an interview with George F. Kennan. The segment was entitled " 'Mr. X,' " a reference to the famous Kennan foreign policy document of 1947 which helped lead to the Truman Doctrine. Igor Oganesoff was the producer and Dan Rather the interviewer. Kennan spoke of fifty years of involvement with Soviet-American relations. Kennan spoke of denying the inevitability of war and declined to dismiss out of hand the Reagan suggestion of a blockade of Cuba as a response to the Soviet invasion of Afghanistan. Kennan denied our nation was on the brink of World War III, but Rather's questions were uncharacteristically pedestrian. Usually Rather is better briefed.

Ross Perot was not the only third-party or Independent candidate for President in the late twentieth century. In 1980 Congressman John Anderson, formerly an Illinois Republican, ran a campaign, and a segment produced by Norman Gorin, "Anderson of Illinois," was narrated by Morley Safer. Anderson endorsed ratification of the Equal Rights Amendment and spoke of sacrifice. Anderson said of Ronald Reagan that he was unconcerned about Reagan's age but rather about the age of his ideas. Reagan of course had been interviewed on an earlier segment.

IRAN, QADAFFI, GOLDWATER
AND AFGHANISTAN

On March 2, 1980, Mike Wallace introduced the Barry Lando production "The Iran File," which traced from a 1976 interview by Wallace with Shah Reza Pahlevi the development of the crisis which led to imprisonment of more than fifty American hostages in Teheran after the raid on the American Embassy there.

Wallace interviewed Raji Samghabdi, who described torture methods allegedly used by the Savak (Iranian secret police). Wallace also spoke with Max McCarthy, the 1976 press officer at the American Embassy. Jesse Leaf, Iran analyst for the CIA in Langley, Virginia, told of being ordered not to write a report on Savak torture methods. Nasser Afshar, publisher of the *Iran Free Press*, told of his fear of the Savak. Joseph Sisco, a Kissinger subordinate who in 1980 was chancellor of the American University in Washington, argued that the United States had made it possible for twenty-five years for Iran to make progress toward being a modern state. Wallace quoted Iranian President Bani-Sadr as saying he was puzzled why Americans did not understand the Iranian revolution. Sisco told Wallace that "six Presidents and six Secretaries of State just can't be totally wrong." The rest of the segment was an update of the continuing hostage situation as of the air date.

Veteran Republican leader Barry Goldwater of Arizona, the 1964 nominee of the GOP for the presidency, was interviewed March 9 by Harry Reasoner. Goldwater argued that Richard Nixon hurt the Republican party and America, and "frankly I don't think he should ever be forgiven." Goldwater also felt Jimmy Carter was the almost sure nominee of the Democrats in 1980. Goldwater's suggestion for the Middle East was "that we might destroy the refinery at Abadan." Goldwater also supported President Carter's policy in Afghanistan. The program was chiefly an exposition of Goldwater's views. No serious effort was made to refute them.

One of the more controversial segments Dan Rather completed during his entire time with "60 Minutes" was aired April 6, 1980. It was "Inside Afghanistan," produced by Andrew Lack, later president of NBC News. Controversy arose about the disguise Rather used to get into Afghanistan, and of course it was related to the disappointment of other correspondents who did not get there first. Rather noted aircraft going into and out of the base at Jalalabad. He spoke through an interpreter to a guerrilla leader named Yassini. Weapons were discussed and a government information officer was interviewed. This was one of the more memorable "beats" scored by Rather before he left to become "CBS Evening News" anchor to succeed Walter Cronkite. Others interviewed were Gulbadin Hikmatyar, formerly of Kabul University, and an Afghan refugee named Mujahdee.[21]

Analysis of programming on "60 Minutes" from late 1980 through 1993 will be considered in Chapter Three.

NOTES

1. Material drawn from Mike Wallace and Gary Paul Gates, *Close Encounters: Mike Wallace's Own Story* (New York: William Morrow and Co., 1984), pp. 1–82.

2. Harry Reasoner, *Before the Colors Fade* (Boston: Little, Brown, 1981); Morley Safer, *Flashbacks: On Returning to Vietnam* (New York: Random House, 1990).

3. Richard Campbell, *60 Minutes and the News: A Mythology for Middle America* (Urbana: University of Illinois Press, 1991).

4. Wallace and Gates, *op. cit.*, pp. 132–152.

5. *Ibid.*, pp. 152–162.
6. *Ibid.*, pp. 159–182.
7. *Ibid.*, pp. 184–212.
8. *Ibid.*
9. *Ibid.*, pp. 247–268.
10. *Ibid.*, pp. 246–342.
11. *Ibid.*, p. 353.
12. *Ibid.*, pp. 358, 359.
13. *Ibid.*, p. 361.
14. *Ibid.*, pp. 361, 362.
15. *Ibid.*, pp. 362, 363.
16. *Ibid.*, pp. 364, 365.
17. CBS News, *60 Minutes Verbatim: Who Said What to Whom: The Complete Text of 114 Stories with Mike Wallace, Morley Safer, Dan Rather, Harry Reasoner* (New York: Arno Press/CBS News, 1980).
18. For information on the anthologies see the following: CBS/Fox Video, *The Best of 60 Minutes, Vol. One* (1984); CBS/Fox Video, *The Best of 60 Minutes, Vol. Two* (1985); Video Yesteryear (Video Images), June 5, 1957; "See It Now," Edward R. Murrow Television Collection (CBS News/Fox Video, 1993), including the following: Edward R. Murrow, "The Best of 'Person to Person' with Connie Chung"; Edward R. Murrow, "The Best of 'See It Now' with Mike Wallace"; Edward R. Murrow, " 'The McCarthy Years' with Walter Cronkite"; Edward R. Murrow, " 'Harvest of Shame' with Dan Rather" (Nos. 5891, 5892, 5899 and 5898). Also see Golden TV Classics, " 'See It Now,' Starring Edward R. Murrow: The Hydrogen Bomb" (1986) (from 1950s program).
19. Full citations of these cases are as follows: *Regents of the University of California v. Bakke* (438 U.S. Reports 265) (1970); *De Funis et al. v. Odegard et al.* (416 U.S. 312) (1974); *U.S. v. Weber et al.* (439 U.S. 1045) (1979).
20. Bob Schieffer and Gary Paul Gates, *The Acting President* (New York: E. P. Dutton, 1989).
21. See Dan Rather, with Mickey Herskowitz, *The Camera Never Blinks Twice* (New York: William Morrow and Company, 1994), pp. 29–61, 64–88.

Chapter Three

Trends away from Traditional Documentaries

Media critic Edwin Diamond noted that Burton Benjamin of CBS felt a serious, detailed examination of a "serious" topic was losing out to fast-paced ratings successes like the CBS hit "60 Minutes" and its ABC counterpart "20/20." In this comment, the CBS veteran termed the network documentary an "endangered species."[1] The comment quoted by Diamond was made at the University of Pennsylvania in February 1987.

Diamond in the same analysis has termed another CBS program, "48 Hours," an "antidocumentary,"[2] in the sense that it is the opposite of the traditional documentary. An analysis of "48 Hours" is found in Chapter Five.

Diamond suggests that "60 Minutes," "20/20" and the other magazine programs "normally offer more infotainment than an exposé or social criticism."[3]

In the same study Diamond notes that CBS "invented the [magazine] form in 1967 and the program continued to roll on into the 1990s."[4] Diamond gives the example of a "60 Minutes" segment on Roy Cohn during which Cohn denied having AIDS while he was being treated at the National Institutes of Health.[5]

A great deal of political content can be found in the January 20, 1991, broadcast of "60 Minutes," as recorded on the CBS transcript. Segments dealt with Saddam Hussein's bodyguard, Captain Karim (a pseudonym), interviewed in Paris by Morley Safer; with an arms dealer, Sarkis Soghanalian, interviewed by Steve Kroft; with Dr. Abdullah Toukhan, science adviser to King Hussein of Jordan, interviewed by Mike Wallace (along with several weapons scientists); and with Vince Cannistrano, former head of counterintelligence for the Central Intelligence Agency, who described the Iraqi terrorists' activity in the United States.

These examples tend to illustrate a charge made by other media critics that the networks tend to rely heavily on individuals who have expertise in a given subject.

Other political segments early in 1991 included a segment on January 6, 1991, in which an exploration was made of psychiatric casualties in the Gulf War; also an interview was conducted with a thirteen-year-old who was tried for murder as an adult. These were shown under the respective titles of "Shell Shock" and "Old Enough to Kill." Were these "infotainment" or were they serious profiles? Such a determination would have to be made on a case by case basis.

On January 13, 1991, a segment on "Iraqi Terror" discussed the Iraqi terrorist threat to the United States (reflecting widespread apprehension at that time). The determination of bias in wartime is particularly hard to measure given the context of such broadcasts. In the print era much attention was given during World War I to newspaper accounts of the sacking of the Louvain Library. In any war by definition there could be atrocities committed by both sides. But in the context of wartime coverage it is difficult for the media in a belligerent country to adhere to the standard of balanced coverage.

Another segment unrelated to the Gulf War dealt with tactics used by the Department of Energy to fight workmen's compensation suits under the title "Body Snatchers?" Such matters cause complicated problems for media coverage because of the constraints normally applied by the judicial system in handling pending cases. Even after settlement of such cases, it is possible that the media will have to contend with courts' gag orders and sealed documents.

On October 21, 1990, a segment, "Iran, Iraq and the U.S.," told how the Iranians believe the United States is secretly in cahoots with Saddam Hussein, their enemy in the eight-year Iran-Iraq War, and "Ward 5A" was a story about the dedication of nurses in the AIDS ward at San Francisco General Hospital, a public institution.

The fact that the United States Senate voted in February 1993 to continue a ban on admission of AIDS victims into the United States illustrates the controversy surrounding the second segment. The first segment illustrates how long suspicion can linger, given the fact that the major confrontation between the United States and Iran occurred during the 1979–1981 hostage crisis.

On October 28, 1990, an interview segment titled "Salman Rushdie" was done with the author of *The Satanic Verses*, who was driven into hiding by an Iranian death penalty in absentia. Rushdie's concealment made taping of the segment difficult for obvious reasons. Another segment, "Who Killed George Polk?" was about a new book about the 1940s murder of a CBS correspondent in Greece. The segment on the Polk case parallels the investigation regarding the murder of Don Bolles, an Arizona correspondent who was publishing exposé material. A similar case occurred in West Virginia in the early 1990s when a journalist was found dead in a hotel after announcing to other people that he was researching a government scandal.

Other "60 Minutes" segments during this period included "The Temple Mount Killings," on December 2, 1990, an investigation into what really happened in the Jerusalem conflict between Arabs and Israelis, and "Dutch Treat II," about the debate in the Netherlands over legalizing brothels. The Arab-Israeli conflict is one of those news stories in which it is apparently impossible to satisfy one side or the other with the nature of coverage. However, opposing sides of the dispute were touched on. Although the Dutch story generated controversy, it was not of the same degree.

On the January 27, 1991, broadcast of "60 Minutes," General Norman Schwarzkopf was interviewed. The commander of Allied troops in the Persian Gulf was questioned by David Martin, CBS Pentagon correspondent. Schwarzkopf confessed that his "worst fear" was that "we would be forced to do something that would cause us to lose the lives of our forces and we'd end up with nothing to show for it." The matter of coverage of military matters is a tricky problem for the press because of the insider/outsider dichotomy. Many lessons learned in Vietnam gave the Pentagon the upper hand in the 1991 coverage.[6] Already several book-length studies have been published in addition to numerous articles.[7]

Along these same lines, Steve Kroft conducted a January 27, 1991, interview with Dr. Jan Medime, a chemical warfare expert, on the possibility that the Iraqis might use poison gas in a ground war against the Allied forces. The same program included a segment entitled "The Secret of the Gara Mountains," an update of an Ed Bradley interview originally aired November 4, 1990. On the segment "The Best Stuff," Morley Safer analyzed the Israeli Air Force and interviewed an Israeli base commander and two pilots as well as General Yarif of the Israeli Air Force. The same general comments mentioned previously apply to the Kroft and Bradley segments.

Also on January 27, 1991, in a segment entitled "Iran, Iraq and the U.S." Mike Wallace interviewed Iranian citizens about their attitudes toward Iraq and the United States. This did not involve public opinion data but was an impressionistic effort to read focus group–type samplings. In a final segment, "Saddam," Wallace interviewed Professor Amazia Bar-Am of Haifa University about the nature of the Iraqi dictator. Analyzing the traits of Saddam could of course call for psychiatric profiling as well as political psychology study of power motivations. This is a slippery kind of problem because of the use of secondhand information.

Topics on the February 10, 1991, broadcast of "60 Minutes" included "The Saudis" (Ed Bradley's interview of Arabian fighting men); Steve Kroft's segment on "Jane's," an interview with the publishing director of the British publication *Jane's*, which analyzes military organizations around the world; a Morley Safer segment, "Tuning In," about the propaganda listening activities of intelligence organizations such as the BBC Monitoring Service (sometimes employed by the CIA); and the segment "Red Cross Blood," which included Meredith Vieira's interviews with Red Cross officials about preparations of blood supplies in the Persian Gulf. These four segments again raise the expert-layman problem in the fields of military structure and management, intelligence work, and fieldwork in combat zones. It is not really possible to draw conclusions, but one would hope that professional information gatherers would secure the kind of briefing that would make these segments more informative.

A feature of the February 24, 1991, edition of "60 Minutes" was an "Update on the Gulf War" with Mike Wallace interviewing CBS correspondents Dan Rather (in Saudi Arabia), Eric Engberg (also in Saudi Arabia), Betsy Aaron (in Baghdad), David Martin (at the Pentagon), and Wyatt Andrews (at the White House). Also included were CBS consultants General George Crist (USMC, retired) and Professor Fouad Ajami of the Johns Hopkins University. The correspondent pieces were of course subject to the availability of information (Rather spent a lot of time in the Gulf War doing human interest features on troops). As for the consultants, the networks (not just CBS, but the others of the original Big Three and CNN as well) have been faulted for giving insufficient information about the background of these informants. This is a problem that the time constraints on television exacerbate, but there does appear to be room for improvement in this regard.

The "60 Minutes" broadcast of March 3, 1991, included the segment "Free at Last!" about the release of CBS correspondent Bob Simon and his camera crew by the Iraqis. Ed Bradley interviewed Simon and CBS producer Peter Bluff, as well as CBS News cameraman Robert Alvarez and CBS News soundman Juan Caldera. Later in the same program Mike Wallace interviewed relatives of a family missing in Missouri in a segment entitled "My Family Is Missing." These two segments carried the common theme of searches for missing persons. A whole syndicated program has been built around this theme, as fans of "Unsolved Mysteries" can attest.

The March 24, 1991, "60 Minutes" aired the segment "Saddam's Billions" with a Steve Kroft interview of Jules Kroll, a private investigator who probed into Saddam Hussein's financial empire, and Sheikh Saud Nasir al-Sabah, Kuwaiti Ambassador to the United States. Another segment, "The Numbers Game," included a Morley Safer interview with the Equal Employment Opportunity Commission (EEOC). Mike Wallace in the segment "The Trials of Michael Dowd" interviewed Michael Dowd, an attorney whose career as a defense lawyer has been controversial. The Saddam fortune story reminds one of the coverage of investments by Filipino President Ferdinand Marcos and Mrs. Imelda Marcos in real estate in New York and other places. Historians may learn of the details but journalists seldom do. The EEOC segment dealt with a highly controversial issue in American domestic politics. Minority interests feel that in many instances existing laws are making up for centuries of inequities, while those opposed to such laws feel they impose a "quota" system. Again the problem of balance arises in such pieces. Statements made previously about the difficulty of covering legal matters apply to the Dowd piece. It needs to be explained to the public that grand jury restrictions and the imposition of court "gag orders" sometimes make facts difficult to come by for the media.

REAL ESTATE SCAMS, ABORTION
AND YELTSIN'S VISIT

On April 21, 1992, Steve Kroft interviewed officials of the Resolution Trust Corporation (RTC) in the segment "You Own It!" about
a land speculation bubble in Colorado Springs, Colorado. Another
segment, entitled "War Games," featured a Mike Wallace interview
with Robert Costello, former U.S. Under Secretary of Defense for
Procurement, about American technological research and development. In a third segment, "Suzanne Logan's Story," Meredith
Vieira interviewed Patrick Malone, attorney for Suzanne Logan,
who was disabled in a botched effort at abortion in Maryland. The
RTC interview not only illustrates problems which arise in piecing
together information where courts are involved, but also shows how
difficult it may be to extract information from the bureaucracy. The
second story involved both the defense bureaucracy and the scientific community. It is not necessary to be working on a Manhattan
Project or a major effort such as the Strategic Defense Initiative to
understand how difficult it may be to obtain information and to
put it into perspective from sources involved in such a story. Of
course, the analysis of Persian Gulf conflict coverage indicated the
increased sophistication of military people where public relations
are concerned (compared with those of the Vietnam era), but the
scientific community is hardly known to have a broadly based
instinct for popular opinion.

The abortion story was based on the human interest factor, and
it can be viewed against the backdrop of state laws which were
quite restrictive prior to the 1973 ruling in *Roe v. Wade* and which
have begun to be tightened up again by the states since the *Webster*
case of 1989. This will no doubt be a staple of feature programs for
many years to come. One may note that the Indiana case of Becky
Bell (a young woman who died after a botched abortion) was
covered in February 1991.

The May 12, 1991, "60 Minutes" program opened with the seg-
ment "Clark M. Clifford," in which Mike Wallace interviewed the
Washington superlawyer who became involved in a scandal con-
cerning the Bank of Credit and Commerce International (BCCI). In
"Playing War," Harry Reasoner told about the movie *I'm 12 Years
Old and I'm a Soldier*, which received the 1990 International Emmy
Award. In the segment he interviewed youths fighting in countries
such as Colombia as guerrilla troops. Ed Bradley, in a segment

entitled "Doctor Forman," interviewed Dr. Les Forman, a psychologist at the Life Plus Treatment Center in California, about his work with youths. The Clifford case was about to go to trial after physicians and the courts had engaged in disputatious discussion of how to proceed. In order for Clifford to undergo surgery, the case was severed from that of Robert Altman, an associate of Clifford's. (Altman was acquitted and the case against Clifford was dropped for lack of evidence in 1993.) The segment on Colombian drug wars combined human interest factors with international concern with the drug traffic. The psychologist interview took place only a short while before the April 1992 Los Angeles riots, at a time when there was a great deal of preoccupation with the problem of youths in the inner cities and less than two years before President Clinton's proposal for summer youth training programs.

On June 2, 1991, a "60 Minutes" segment, "RU-486," dealt with the newly developed French abortion pill and the opposition to this medical advance by the right-to-life movement. (Since the segment was broadcast, an executive order was issued by President Clinton in early 1993 indicating that bans on importation of the drug were lifted with efforts of pro-choice groups in the United States to persuade the French developer to export the drug; there was some talk of turning to Chinese sources for this medication.)

A second segment on that date, titled "Underworld," focused on the New York City Transit Authority Police undercover unit concerned with the safety of the subway system. (This occurred prior to the development of a major subterranean safety problem on February 26, 1993, when an explosion disrupted PATH service from New Jersey and the commodities market.) It was a human interest story of the type featured on the more recently developed "Street Stories."

Subjects of "60 Minutes" segments on June 9, 1991, included "This House Is a Steal," an Ed Bradley interview regarding a Florida real estate scam; "Dr. Brooks," a follow-up on a Harry Reasoner interview about Tutwiler, Mississippi, and its medical aid program, and "The Pollards," a Mike Wallace interview with convicted espionage agent Jonathan Pollard, convicted of spying for Israel in the United States, and his defense attorney, Alan Dershowitz, as well as Joseph DiGenova, former U.S. attorney. Real estate scams appear to be a recurring theme on these shows. The Mississippi story indicates how community activism can be of interest around the nation and even around the world.

The June 23, 1991, "60 Minutes" coincided with the visit of Russian Federation President Boris Yeltsin to Washington, D.C. Segments on that program included "Voyage of Discovery," a Mike Wallace interview with Admiral William Crowe, chairman of the Joint Chiefs of Staff, and General Moiseyev, head of the Soviet Armed Forces; "Chernobyl, Moscow, CCCP-TV in Moscow, and Telling the Truth," Mike Wallace, Steve Kroft and Harry Reasoner interviews; "The Moscow Mystique," a Harry Reasoner interview previously completed with Elena Korensvskala; "Yalta," Mike Wallace and Morley Safer interviews; "The Last Gulag," a Mike Wallace interview with prisoners; "Joseph Stalin," Mike Wallace's interview about the late Soviet dictator, and "Slava," a Mike Wallace interview with Mstislav Rostropovich, music director of Washington's National Symphony Orchestra (NSO).

The reciprocal visits by Admiral Crowe (in 1993 a consultant to President Clinton) and General Moiseyev represented a part of what used to be called the "thaw" between East and West. These segments preceded by only a couple of months the abortive anti-Gorbachev coup of late summer 1991. Environmental concerns and their coverage in 1991 were the focus of the Chernobyl segment; Chernobyl had been a major worry of the international environmental movement since 1986. The Korensvskala interview has already been mentioned; "Yalta" dealt with a Crimean resort area which was the scene of a widely disputed conference late in World War II involving Roosevelt, Churchill and Stalin. It has been a rest and recreation area for Russian leaders. The Gulag piece focused on prisoners in the prison camps (many in Siberia) about which Alexandr Solzhenitsyn, a monarchist, wrote in the 1950s and 1960s. The Stalin interview indicates that historically important figures cast a long shadow as Stalin died in 1953 just prior to the negotiation of the Korean truce. Ostensibly, Rostropovich as a musician would appear to be non-political, but the fact is that he was a friend of Andrei Sakharov, the scientist forced into internal exile during the Brezhnev regime in a sort of "mirror image" of the experience of J. Robert Oppenheimer in the United States in the 1950s (Oppenheimer was not sent into exile but he retired to the Center for Advanced Studies at Princeton University after having his security clearance lifted during the Eisenhower years; he was a leader in the Manhattan Project in World War II). After this segment was aired, the cellist "Slava" announced his pending retirement and scheduled return to Russia after leaving the NSO in 1994.

ABORTION NOTIFICATION VICTIM AND
THE SALMAN RUSHDIE CASE

On July 14, 1991, "60 Minutes" contained two segments which had political significance. The first of these, "Becky's Story," consisted of a Morley Safer interview with the parents of Becky Bell, who died as a result of a botched abortion in Indiana, which has a parental notification law regarding abortions. The segment was an update of a February 1991 report on the Bell case. The parents say Becky was forced into a back alley abortion and they are opposing parental consent laws, which were recently defeated in nine of ten states where they were proposed. This is a part of the social issue agenda in which abortion is a recurring theme, because of the context of the national debate over abortion. From a network standpoint it is practically impossible to present a balanced view on so controversial a topic as abortion, the late twentieth century's moral equivalent of the pre–Civil War slavery issue, in the opinion of many. But public interest in the subject obliged networks to provide coverage. It is a thorny matter.

On July 21, 1991, a segment entitled "Salman Rushdie" covered the frustrating experiences of the author of *The Satanic Verses*, whose earlier in absentia death sentence for what was termed blasphemy was renewed by Islamic religious authorities in 1993. The courts of Iran, in the post-revolutionary period run by the religious leaders, pronounced this sentence.

A politically controversial Hollywood producer and director, Oliver Stone, was the object of a July 28 segment entitled "Oliver's Story" examining the career of the producer of *JFK* and *Platoon*. The first movie dealt with the controversy over a possible conspiracy in the Kennedy assassination of 1963, and the second with the Vietnam conflict. This interview was conducted by Morley Safer. The Kennedy assassination was the object of renewed interest after the movie's release; it was the subject of numerous video releases which were followed up by another 1992 release about the life of Malcolm X, another assassinated figure from the 1960s.

On August 4, 1991, Mike Wallace conducted interviews with a family whose members became involved in KGB espionage for the Soviet Union. This segment, "The Walkers," was about a Navy family, John Walker, his wife, a son in the Navy, a daughter in the Army, and his brother, a retired naval officer. The Walker family had been the subject of a television movie, *Family of Spies* (based on the book by that name), presented about a month earlier. John Walker, now serving a prison term, told Mike Wallace about the motivation for his confessed espionage.

Steve Kroft in the segment "Acid Rain" on the August 4 program interviewed Dr. James Mahoney, director of the National Acid Precipitation Assessment Program, as well as Senator Daniel Patrick Moynihan (D-New York), who has followed the issue in Congress. Others interviewed by Kroft were David Hawkins, lobbyist for the National Resources Defense Council; Senator John Glenn (D-Ohio); Robert Murray, owner of the Ohio Valley Coal Company; and syndicated columnist Warren Brookes. The interviews brought opposing views of the acid rain problem. Like the coverage of Chernobyl and Three Mile Island in earlier times, the acid rain controversy dealt with environmental themes. The acid rain controversy also has international overtones, as became apparent in the Rio de Janeiro global environmental conference of 1992 in which the position of the United States as stated by the Bush administration drew fire from various less developed countries (LDCs).

On August 11, 1991, Steve Kroft conducted a "60 Minutes" follow-up of a March segment, "Saddam's Billions," and updated the information from the March interview. This was of course also a follow-up on the Gulf War coverage; further involvement of the Middle East in the news came in February 1993 with speculation of possible involvement of Middle Eastern patrons in the bombing of the New York World Trade Center. The defendants in this case were convicted in March 1994.

The "60 Minutes" program for August 25, 1991, included two segments with political significance. The first, entitled "What Now?," covered current conditions in the former Soviet Union. Mike Wallace conducted an interview with a young Russian reporter, Artyom Borovik, who concluded, "We're in the middle of a civil war. . . . Tomorrow might bring surprises. We have about a year. We democrats have about a year ahead to prove that we are able to solve these problems, and if this year passes and we haven't proven that, we might face another coup." The theme of international relations has provided another staple of the "60 Minutes" agenda, as witness the Walker spy segment referred to previously, as well as the coverage of the Gulf War and its aftermath.

A segment of the September 1, 1991, program entitled "War Games" updated a report on the Gulf War and the use of Patriot missiles therein. President George Bush described the Patriot missiles as "a triumph of American technology," and Mike Wallace's interview brought out the views of Richard Solomon, a researcher at the Massachusetts Institute of Technology (MIT), on the importance of continuing research into weapons systems as a result of the Persian Gulf War experience. This segment continued a theme going back all the way to the 1970s coverage of "The Pentagon Papers" and the controversial documentary "The Selling of the Pentagon."

An unusual segment was included in the September 8, 1991, "60 Minutes." An interview by Morley Safer with Artyom Borovik, entitled "Room 19," told of the preservation by the Soviets of the brains of Lenin and Stalin as well as other prominent Soviet leaders. This developed the theme of new trends in Gorbachev's Russia. This theme would be picked up on numerous times in the weeks and months to follow.

WHITE-COLLAR CRIME, THE POISON UMBRELLA AND PROZAC

The September 22, 1991, "60 Minutes" contained two politically significant segments. The first, "The Secret Life of Dennis Levine," dealt with Wall Street scandals and enforcement problems of the Securities and Exchange Commission (SEC) in the U.S. Department of Justice. Ed Bradley interviewed Dennis Levine, a former highly paid stockbroker, who confessed to violation of the securities act while working for a Wall Street brokerage firm. The Bradley interview with Mr. Levine ended with the following quote from Levine: "I . . . don't think I've done anything wrong."

The theme of white-collar crime was a pervasive one during the 1980s. Other securities frauds involving such individuals as Ivan Boesky, Michael Milken and other Wall Street figures were the object of scrutiny, along with land scam figures, unlicensed training schools, "blue sky" entrepreneurs and the like.

One segment on September 29, 1991, "The KGB," was introduced by Lesley Stahl, who described an interview conducted in Moscow by Artyom Borovik, special CBS correspondent, with former KGB agents Colonel Mikhail Petrovich Lubemov, General Vstislav Artyomov and General Boris Solamatin. In one interview, Colonel Lubemov charged that it was "not the United States, but the KGB, that was now the enemy of the Russian people," and claimed that "the KGB had been plotting to destroy the Russian president, Boris Yeltsin, by spreading disinformation about his drinking and womanizing." The Borovik special segment included a visit to the KGB's infamous Lubyenka Prison in Moscow.

This segment is part of a larger agenda of security related investigations reflecting broad public interest in foreign policy matters at that time. For a long time much of the material about the KGB was classified, and the availability of some of these interview subjects was relatively novel.

The October 20, 1991, "60 Minutes" included a Mike Wallace interview segment introduced by Ed Bradley, "The 'Trashing' of Clayton Hartwig." This portion of the broadcast dealt with efforts by the U.S. Navy to blame Gunner's Mate Clayton Hartwig for triggering an explosion on the battleship *Iowa*. These efforts ended October 17, 1991, with an apology by Admiral Frank Kelso, Chief of Naval Operations, who later resigned because of Operation Tailgate; the Admiral apologized to Hartwig's family and stated that the cause of the explosion could not be established.

The controversy over the military policy regarding the rules of conduct concerning homosexuals was involved in the Hartwig case. This involved litigation begun by the explosion victim's family. The controversy erupted all over again when in January 1993 President Bill Clinton proposed an order lifting the ban (then–Secretary of Defense Les Aspin warned flag officers that the courts were likely to act even if the President did not). The courts also dealt with suits filed by aggrieved parties in the civil courts on the issue.

Morley Safer conducted the interview on another October 20 segment, "Minister of Foreign Affairs," covering reports about Italy's Minister of Foreign Affairs, Gianni de Michaelis, which began with Safer's declaration: "This 52-year-old mountain of a man believes that being in public life is no reason to stop a man from living the good life." The term "good life" refers to the minister's alleged liaisons with beautiful Italian women.

This interview reflected the "soft news" approach by focusing on a major figure in the Italian government but dealing with interest in his off-duty activities. This kind of reporting has been controversial in media coverage of American politics as well (e.g., the Gary Hart campaign), and controversies have surrounded several other political figures.

Morley Safer followed a Lesley Stahl segment on the FDA and the drug Prozac with another October 27, 1991, module, "Texas

Rules," consisting of an interview with Governor Ann Richards of Texas and her background of political experience prior to becoming Governor of the Lone Star State. Governor Richards attracted national attention in 1988 at the Democratic National Convention in Atlanta when she said that "George Bush was born with a silver foot in his mouth." The interview noted that Governor Richards learned a great deal about politics from President Lyndon B. Johnson and entered politics during the 1960 John F. Kennedy presidential campaign.

Governor Richards, one of the first women to serve as elected governor of a major state, drew much attention from both print and electronic media in her first months as Texas chief executive. She was in the news again in March 1993 when a shootout at a religious compound of the Branch Davidians near Waco left several Alcohol, Tobacco and Firearms (ATF) agents of the Treasury Department dead or wounded when the David Koresh cult proved to have an arsenal of deadly weapons. (Though not convicted of conspiracy, some of the cultists were convicted of lesser charges in 1994.) The standoff at Waco was resolved eventually by a fire which took the lives of most of the cultists in the compound; the standoff and its grim conclusion were the object of much network attention as well as major newsmagazine articles.

Ed Bradley conducted an interview on the November 3, 1991, "60 Minutes" in a module entitled "No MSG." This dealt with a study of the effects of monosodium glutamate conducted at the Eastern Virginia Medical School. The FDA has agreed with the food industry that MSG poses no health problems, according to Bradley's segment.

This item is another on the health care agenda, in a fashion similar to the Prozac topic previously referred to. The health care issue was a major concern during the 1992 presidential campaign and attracted much attention to proposed Clinton legislation well into his term.

The "60 Minutes" for November 10, 1991, contained a module called "Friendly Fire" featuring an investigation and interviews by Steve Kroft into the way in which thirty-five American troops in the Persian Gulf conflict were killed by "friendly fire" from their own forces. Kroft interviewed Lt. Col. Ralph Hales of the U.S. Army, who was a part of the incident. Kroft also questioned the family of Jeff Middleton, an Oxford, Kansas, corporal who was one of the victims, and the mother of Robert Talley, of Newark, New

Jersey, another soldier killed by friendly fire. Kroft noted that "last May, General Gordon Sullivan, the Army chief of staff, ordered a special task force to begin looking into ways to reduce friendly fire casualties. That task force is still at work."

The controversy over friendly fire casualties results from the confusion and clamor which usually surround a battlefield situation. No one has maintained that such incidents occur through other than accidental events, but interest was sufficient to inspire the publication of a book, *Friendly Fire* by G.D.F. Bryant, about an incident during the Vietnam conflict. That book was later made into a network television movie starring Carol Burnett as the aggrieved mother of the soldier killed in Vietnam. That such a movie was made illustrates the blurring between "entertainment" programming and "soft news" programming.

NORPLANT, CORPORATE PAY AND
IRAQI NUCLEAR DEVELOPMENT

Ed Bradley on November 10, 1991, in "Norplant," discussed a birth control method (Norplant) and the constitutional controversy surrounding the effort to introduce it into the United States. Bradley noted that one judge ordered the use of this method to sterilize a Tulare, California, woman named Darlene Johnson. Bradley interviewed Judge Howard Broadman and State Representative Cary Patrick of Kansas, also involved in a separate controversy in that state. He proposed a bill that would pay women $500 to use Norplant; the bill was opposed by State Representative Kathleen Sebillas, who said in an interview with Bradley that she found this procedure repugnant. Bradley ended his report thus: "Cary Patrick's bill will be taken up by the Kansas legislature this winter. In an initial vote last spring, the bill was defeated. However, a provision was passed making Norplant available free to any woman on welfare in Kansas."

The whole Norplant decision controversy ties in with the national pro-choice versus pro-life controversy. The item is another on the health care agenda referred to earlier in the discussion of the Prozac module and the RU-486 pill developed by French pharmaceutical manufacturers.

The November 17, 1991, "60 Minutes" featured a segment entitled "Saddam's Secrets" with interviews by Mike Wallace regarding the Iraqi nuclear development program put under United Nations surveillance after the Persian Gulf conflict. Wallace interviewed Dr. David Kay, an American engineer who was knowledgeable about the Iraqi nuclear weapons development program. Wallace noted that "Kay and his men have the right to search anywhere any time in Iraq." The segment also included a Wallace interview with Ken Timmerman, author of *The Death Lobby*, which details Saddam's acquisition of his military capability. The International Atomic Energy Agency (IAEA) of the United Nations, even prior to the Gulf conflict, had been sending inspectors into Iraq as it does into almost sixty countries.

This item was a part of the Gulf conflict coverage on which programs in 1991 concentrated, particularly in the early part of the year, but on a continuing basis in the conflict's aftermath as people examined the ongoing struggle in the region.

On a November 17 module, "The Psycho Squad," in an interview by Lesley Stahl with FBI agent John Douglas, the correspondent visited the FBI Academy at Quantico, Virginia, and learned about an FBI unit which seeks to explore the minds of serial killers and rapists. Agent Douglas cited the example of Jeffrey Dahmer, the Milwaukee serial killer who mutilated his victims.

This module combined the criminal justice agenda item with the health care item in its concern with the issue of mental health and its impact on criminal behavior. It was therefore focused on a social issue of major importance.

On the "60 Minutes" broadcast for November 24, 1991, Steve Kroft in a segment, "The Teamsters," interviewed William McCarthy, the former Teamsters Union president, about reform of the union. Kroft also interviewed three candidates for Teamsters president, Ron Carey, international vice president Ralph Vincent "R. V." Durham, and Walter Shea.

This module preceded by only about a year the release of *Hoffa*, a motion picture about the life and career of James R. Hoffa, the Robert F. Kennedy nemesis whose mysterious disappearance has been a topic of speculation ever since it occurred in the 1970s. Unions as much as management and government are a part of reform efforts in the 1990s, and this interest prompted significant audience reaction to this segment.

On the December 15, 1991, "60 Minutes," Ed Bradley investigated the controversy over the Food and Drug Administration (FDA) approval of the drug Halcion used as a sleeping pill. The controversy resulted from a decision by British authorities to ban

Halcion in the United Kingdom. Bradley interviewed Dr. Anthony Kales of Penn State University and Dr. Graham Dukes of the Dutch drug regulatory agency about their views of the Halcion danger. In another interview, Dr. Theodore Cooper, Upjohn Pharmaceuticals chairman, defended the drug's use in proper dosages. Bradley also referred to a BBC interview with Dr. Robert Straw, Upjohn director of project management, who described clinical trials of the contro-versial drug. Bradley closed by noting: "I recently got a letter from Upjohn suggesting I had moderated a panel discussion for family physicians on the subject of sleep disorders, a panel that . . . was funded by one of Upjohn's rivals. Had I believed that constituted a conflict, I wouldn't have done this story." (This segment of course preceded the widely touted Harry and Louise commercials spon-sored early in 1994 by the drug industry.)

The Halcion controversy was added to the list of medically related issues covered on "60 Minutes," along with RU-486 and Prozac. This is a recurring agenda item for "60 Minutes," as dem-onstrated by the 1991 coverage.

In "Hussein and Hussein" on December 22, 1991, Steve Kroft discussed the relationship between Iraqi strongman Saddam Hussein and King Hussein of Jordan. Kroft interviewed Ahmed Challaby, a leader of the Iraqi resistance movement, who discussed how vital the support and assistance of King Hussein and the Jordanian people were for Saddam's survival and success. Challaby noted that the U.S. State Department has been reluctant to pressure King Hussein because of his assistance in setting up the Madrid process for the Middle Eastern Peace Conference.

The conference was launched in Madrid and since then discus-sions have been held in several different locations, including Wash-ington, D.C. The talks were interrupted in 1992 at the time of the deportation of Palestinians accused of Intifada violence by the Israeli government. The discussions were eventually restarted and ended with the signing of a peace agreement in Washington, D.C., in September 1993. The implementation of this agreement in the Middle East has been complicated, but not totally ended, by such incidents as the Hebron mosque massacre of 1994.

The analysis of leadership styles of foreign leaders and their impact on the relationship of various nations in diplomacy has been a recurring theme in the "60 Minutes" repertoire. The earlier dis-cussion of the research done about Stalin and Lenin was another example of this, in addition to the 1992 discussions of leadership styles of Bush, Clinton and Perot.

The December 29, 1991, "60 Minutes" broadcast opened with a segment by Lesley Stahl entitled "Georgia"; she interviewed President Zviad Gamsakhurdia of the former Soviet republic of Georgia, now independent, whose opposition finally succeeded in replacing him with Eduard Shevardnadze after September 1991. Gamsakhurdia told Stahl, "We have more freedom here, more freedom than the United States, because here is anarchy." Stahl also interviewed the opposition leader Lana Gogbradize, a well-known film director in Georgia, who charged of the Gamsakhurdia regime: "It is a simple dictatorship." Stahl also interviewed opposition leader Dr. Tomori Chachkiani, who said of the strongman: "He supported Georgian independence, but seems unconcerned with the concept of human rights and freedom of the press. He misses the old sense of order." In this interview he described Gamsakhurdia as a great admirer of Stalin.

Continuing interest in the former Soviet Union is reflected in this segment. All through the year's programming, the area was the focus of attention as major changes occurred in the former Soviet republics which had just gained independence.

The preceding program segments illustrate some of the problems of producing credible material on magazine programs.[8] They also show how in the prime time environment it is sometimes difficult to define programs clearly as news or entertainment.[9]

The variety of stories carried on "60 Minutes" during the 1991 calendar year demonstrates how many political situations it has reported on and the human interest aspects of these stories.[10] This also demonstrates why "60 Minutes" has a consistently high viewership, a matter which will be dealt with in greater detail in Chapter Nine.

NOTES

1. Edwin Diamond, *The Media Show: The Changing Face of the News, 1985–1990* (Cambridge: MIT Press, 1991), p. 29.

2. *Ibid.*, p. 31.

3. *Ibid.*, p. 39.

4. *Ibid.*, pp. 66, 67.

5. *Ibid.*, p. 91.

6. See Robert E. Denton, Jr., ed., *The Media and the Persian Gulf War* (Westport,

CT: Praeger, 1993); Marcia Lynn Whicker, James P. Pfiffner and Raymond A. Moore, eds., *The Presidency and the Persian Gulf War* (Westport, CT: Praeger, 1993); and Martha Joynt Kumar, *Wired for Sound and Pictures: The President and White House Communications Policies* (Baltimore: The Johns Hopkins University Press, forthcoming).

7. Some of the literature on this subject includes Ken Auletta, *Three Blind Mice: How the TV Networks Lost Their Way* (New York: Random House, 1991); Reuven Frank, *Out of Thin Air: The Brief Wonderful Life of Network News* (New York: Simon & Schuster, 1991); Robert Slater, *This . . . Is CBS: A Chronicle of 60 Years* (Englewood Cliffs, NJ: Prentice-Hall, 1988); Peter J. Boyer, *Who Killed CBS? The Undoing of America's Number One News Network* (New York: Random House, 1988); Martin A. Lee and Norman Solomon, *Unreliable Sources: A Guide to Detecting Bias in News Media* (New York: Lyle Stuart/Carol Publishing Group, 1991), a leftist critique; and Jude Wanniski, *Repap 1992 Media Guide: A Critical Review of the Media* (Morristown, NJ: Polyconomics, 1992), a conservative critique and assessment of ownership structures and editorial policies.

8. "Off the Air: NBC News President, Burned by Staged Fire and GM, Will Resign," *Wall Street Journal* CCXXI, no. 41 (March 2, 1993), A1, A12.

9. Richard Salant on April 14, 1976, sought to make a distinction between the news and entertainment functions of broadcast, p. ii, Preface, *CBS News Standards*.

10. All references to content of broadcasts are based on transcripts purchased from Burrelle's Transcripts, Livingston, New Jersey, and from transcribed tapes of the broadcasts analyzed. Details may be found in the Appendices.

Chapter Four

Content Analysis of 1992 "60 Minutes" Programs

The 1992 "60 Minutes" broadcasts included numerous segments with political significance, as the following examples indicate.

A January 5, 1992, "Time Bombs" segment narrated by Morley Safer dealt with efforts to get rid of chemical weapons in the United States and the former Soviet Union. Safer interviewed General Harry Karegeannes at a Utah storage site. Karegeannes cautioned that great care should be used in moving stored chemical weapons from storage sites to other locations. Safer also interviewed Dr. Matthew Meselson, a Harvard University scientist, who said it was never determined how to destroy such weapons; General Walter Busby, program manager for the Chemical Weapons Demilitarization Program, who spoke of the difficulty of destroying weapons; Charles and Kathy Flood, protestors against the building at a Kentucky site of an incinerator to destroy the weapons; and General Mersyn Jackson, an emergency planner in Kentucky, who was working on the incinerator project. The segment, which provided some useful information, did analyze some problems found with disarmament in this arms industry category. It was analytical and informative, as a good module should be.

Also on January 5, Lesley Stahl did a series of interviews on "Children of the Berlin Wall" which dealt with children removed from their parents by the former East German government. Stahl interviewed Gabriele Yonan, a survivor of the Communist regime in the former East Germany; Jurgen Schmidt, a spokesman for the current German Ministry of Justice, who described the forced adoption policy in the former East Germany; Werner Grahm, a former East German Communist who adopted one of the children; Heike Soldman, whose child was seized by the Communist regime; Jeannette Grubel, an adopted child who did not know hers was a forced adoption; and Arne Grahm, also adopted. This informative sequence gave much useful background information; it shed light on a little known aspect of the Communist regime's repression in the former East Germany.

The January 12, 1992, "60 Minutes" began with the segment "Black Market Babies"; Mike Wallace investigated a Memphis, Tennessee, story in which with the connivance of a corrupt judge a black market in babies was operated in the 1940s. Wallace interviewed parents and children affected by the "ring"; he also interviewed Judge Robert Taylor, a Tennessee jurist who delved into the conspiracy to promote illegal adoptions. This informative segment sought to present both the accuser and accused's stories; thus the CBS guidelines for fairness in presentation were followed.

Morley Safer in a January 12 piece, "Don't Leave Home," dealt with problems in international tourism. Safer described the building of the troubled $4 billion Euro Disney in France and other factors expected to become politically controversial. This segment gave opportunities to be heard to both sides of a controversial subject. It was tightly edited, in general well presented.

Ed Bradley on January 12 limned a "60 Minutes" profile of General Colin Powell, then chairman of the Joint Chiefs of Staff. In an interview, General Powell discussed growing up in the Bronx and why he has shied away from politics despite his highly visible role in the 1991 Persian Gulf conflict. General Powell told Bradley of being "raised with . . . traditional family values." This was some time before the "family values" issue was raised during the 1992 presidential campaign. The interview, while favorable, did attempt to deal with Powell evenhandedly.

Lesley Stahl on the January 19, 1992, "60 Minutes" questioned Army Colonel Tom Baker on "The World's Biggest Shopping Spree." He described the Pentagon's East Coast supply system, with expenditures in the billions to supply and store armed forces materials. Stahl also interviewed Robert Molino of the Defense Logistics Agency and Frank Conahan of the General Accounting Office (GAO) about this costly enterprise. This was informative and a good example of the kind of investigative reporting the public has come to expect from "60 Minutes."

Morley Safer on January 19 completed a segment entitled "Nayirah"; he interviewed a Kuwaiti citizen, Nayirah al-Sabah, who told of Iraqi soldiers coming into hospitals, taking babies out of incubators, taking the incubators, and leaving the infants to die on the cold floor. Safer also interviewed Representative John Porter (R-Illinois), who held hearings into this matter in the U.S. House of Representatives. Amnesty International spokesperson Sean Styles and Andrew Whitley, executive director of the human rights group Middle East Watch, also spoke. Then Safer interviewed *Harper's* magazine publisher John R. MacArthur and Representative Tom Lantos (D-California), as well as Lauri Fitz Pegado of the public relations firm of Hill and Knowlton. These interviews probed into whether Nayirah was the daughter of the Kuwaiti Ambassador to Washington and whether this fact had been improperly concealed (it was concealed during the Persian Gulf conflict because of fear of reprisals against her and her family). Also questioned by Safer was Craig Fuller, George Bush's vice presidential chief of staff and a former president of Hill and Knowlton. This segment provided an interesting question of journalistic ethics and there was some justification for it. It was an interesting and provocative report in the sense that it dealt with a little discussed issue.

DEATH PENALTY, CHILDREN WITH GUNS AND "BUY AMERICAN"

On February 9 in "Buy American" Lesley Stahl investigated commercial competition between the United States and Japan in interviews of officials from the American and Japanese auto industries. The informative piece contributed in a balanced manner to public understanding of an important issue, prominent for several years; much of the public still does not have in-depth knowledge of its many ramifications.

On February 9 in "Mirror, Mirror on the Wall . . ." Steve Kroft dug into the FDA policy of warning against silicone liquid injections as a dangerous cosmetic procedure (as used in breast implants for women). Kroft interviewed Dr. David Kessler, the new FDA commissioner, who said liquid silicone is "an illegal product, and it should not be used." Kroft also interviewed people who had used the product with damaging results. He said the American Academy of Dermatology declined to be interviewed on this subject. It was an informative but alarming report.

On February 16, 1992, in "The Sting," Mike Wallace looked at the prosecution of a Nebraska farmer, Keith Jacobson, accused of receiving a pornographic magazine in the mail and arrested in a "sting." Jacobson, sentenced to perform community service, felt the arrest was an entrapment and appealed his conviction to the United States Supreme Court, where his case was pending at airtime. This part of the program dealt with an important civil liberties issue in the United States—an issue the Supreme Court had considered in several forms many times in the past, and one likely to reappear before the Court in future sessions.

Also on the February 16 "60 Minutes" broadcast, in the segment "Car Seats" Ed Bradley conducted an investigation into the malfunctioning of seat belts in automobiles.

On February 23, 1991, Ed Bradley's "Saddam's Killing Fields" module investigated the persecution of the minority Kurds by the Iraqi government of strongman Saddam Hussein. Andre Whitley, director of the human rights organization Middle East Watch, told Bradley that Kurds, a non-Arab people, were the object of a 1988 massacre by Saddam. Bradley also interviewed Jamal Amin, imprisoned by the Iraqis because he belonged to a political party which sought more self-rule for Kurds. Bradley noted that "a United Nations investigator released a report concluding that the scale of Iraqi human rights violations is almost without parallel since the atrocities committed by the Nazis during World War II." This segment dealt with the difficult task of separating out propaganda in the Gulf War from facts about the enemy Iraqi regime. It appears Bradley did this fairly, but it must have been difficult for him not to caricature Saddam Hussein.[1]

On February 23 Morley Safer in "Life, Death and Politics" examined a Bush-era federal ban on the use of fetal tissue transplants taken from abortion clinics, despite the fact that use of this material has applications in the treatment of Alzheimer's and Parkinson's diseases, diabetes and other genetic illnesses. Safer interviewed the Reverend Guy Walden, pastor of the Broadway Baptist Temple in Houston, who opposes abortion but believes the ban is a mistake. The interview brought out that the ban contributed to the death of Walden's daughter, Angie, who had Hurler's disease. Safer also interviewed Dr. Curt Freed, who performed transplantation of fetal tissue in defiance of the federal ban to treat Parkinson's disease patients. James Brock, attorney for the National Right to Life Committee, favors the ban. He maintained ending the ban would only encourage more abortions. The fact that opposing views were presented reflected an effort, somewhat successful, to give a balanced presentation of a heated and controversial issue.

In another February 23 segment, "Malcolm X," Mike Wallace examined the life and career of civil rights activist Malcolm X. Wallace discussed *The Autobiography of Malcolm X* by the late Alex Haley, with quotations from some of Malcolm X's speeches. Wallace interviewed the African American producer Spike Lee, who produced a Malcolm X film biography starring Denzel Washington (who also starred in historically significant *Glory* and politically significant *Philadelphia*, about an AIDS victim fired by a law firm).

On the March 1, 1992, "60 Minutes," Mike Wallace in "Red Cell" told of a terrorist simulation group led by Dick Marsinco which had "broken into more than 200 highly sensitive U.S. military installations all over the world." Marsinco and his team of U.S. Navy "SEALS" had proved that "real terrorists could capture a U.S. nuclear submarine, take it out to sea, and fire its missiles back at the U.S." The exercise showed how anti-terrorist activities could be run. Thus was explored a relatively little examined corner of the anti-terrorist effort by governments worldwide.

Another March 1 segment was Lesley Stahl's "Dr. Mengele's Laboratory," in which she examined how a Nazi German SS officer, Dr. Josef Mengele, sent tens of thousands of victims to the Auschwitz gas chambers. She interviewed five survivors: Eva Moses, Hans Klein, Kalman Barone, Miriam Moses and Rene Gutman. Stahl noted, "Fifty years after Auschwitz, the stirrings of a new Nazi movement in Germany scare the Mengele twins" (sons of the late Nazi doctor). This was an informative and historically rich reminder of the crimes of the Nazi era in Germany.

Steve Kroft on March 1 examined "The Oregon Plan," in which the state of Oregon is trying to control health care costs. Kroft interviewed Dr. John Kitzhaber, president of the Oregon State Senate and author of the Oregon legislation and an emergency room physician. Through interviews, Kroft spotlighted the work of the Oregon Health Services Commission, which administers the new plan. Kroft talked with U.S. Representative Henry Waxman (D-California), who opposed the plan because it would deny health services to some citizens because of the lack of funds. The segment was a thorough and useful examination of this important issue, which became a top agenda item for the Clinton administration beginning in 1993.

On March 8, 1992, "60 Minutes" opened with a segment in which under the title "Another Karen Silkwood?" Steve Kroft interviewed Linda Porter, a co-worker of Karen Silkwood, the Oklahoma nuclear fuel plant employee who some believe was murdered for becoming a whistle-blower about objectionable plant environmental conditions. Linda Porter worked at the Comanche Peak nuclear power plant near Dallas when it was built. Kroft said Linda Porter "was afraid she might become another Karen Silkwood after discovering that workers there were being exposed to asbestos and other dangerous chemicals."

The final March 8, 1992, regular "60 Minutes" segment, "American Gothic Gone Mad," consisted of Ed Bradley's interviews about Missouri murders related to cattle rustling. He talked to William Webster, Missouri attorney general, about the killings near Springfield; it was claimed that farmer Ray Copeland killed homeless men "because he thought they wouldn't be missed if they disappeared." The case came to a head with a search of Copeland's home, where the missing victims' clothing was found. In his barn they found three bodies buried; all had been shot in the back of the head. Juries convicted both Ray Copeland, scheduled for execution by lethal injection, and his wife, Faye Copeland (a convicted accessory), who was Death Row's oldest woman. He was seventy-six and she was seventy. This report included a good deal of useful background information on a capital punishment case, itself the object of much controversy.

The March 15, 1992, "60 Minutes" began with another story about prisoners, a segment with a Morley Safer interview entitled "Bill and Kathy Swan." The Swans, in prison in Washington State at airtime, were convicted of the violent sexual abuse of their own three-year-old daughter and her three-year-old friend.

JOGGER VIOLENCE CASE, EMILY'S LIST, NARCOTICS AND KISSINGER

On March 15, Mike Wallace's segment, "Yusef Salaam," focused on New York's Central Park crime in which a young woman jogging in the park was attacked and raped by three teenage gang members. Wallace interviewed one of the accused, fifteen-year-old

Yusef Salaam, who denied participating in the crime and said he "never even saw anything." Wallace also interviewed Steve Lopez, a witness to the "wilding" attack (a frenzy of violence) in the park, who contradicted Salaam's story. Wallace noted: "We wanted to ask New York district attorney Robert Morgenthau about all this, the lack of any forensic evidence, the lie detector test, but he declined to say anything and went so far as to prohibit his entire staff from answering our questions because he said the conviction is being appealed." New York City police said they would be glad to talk with Wallace but Morgenthau had gagged them pending the appeal. Wallace attempted to avoid bias by interviewing both sides in the case.

Morley Safer conducted interviews on an informational segment of the March 22, 1992, "60 Minutes" entitled "Emily's List," which described the activities of a fund-raising group to elect women to public office begun by Ellen Malcolm and based on the phrase "Early money is like yeast." The group, which seeks to elect pro-choice candidates, had some success in 1992. Safer interviewed Ellen Malcolm to bring out how the organization had assisted Governor Ann Richards of Texas and Senator Barbara Mikulski (D-Maryland) in their campaigns. He also noted the impact of Professor Anita Hill's testimony in the Clarence Thomas (Supreme Court justice nominee) hearings in 1991.

The March 29, 1992, "60 Minutes" led with a module about former Secretary of State Henry Kissinger entitled "Kissinger" narrated by Mike Wallace. It was noteworthy for Kissinger's refusal to submit to an interview by Wallace (at the time Kissinger was a member of the CBS Board of Directors); Wallace put together the segment by using public statements and previous Kissinger interviews. The subject matter consisted chiefly of information and allegations about Kissinger's highly paid consulting activities since his retirement from government service.

Wallace ended the Kissinger module as follows:

Henry Kissinger declined to sit for an interview unless we went along with his ground rules, ground rules about controlling the editing that have been traditionally unacceptable on "60 Minutes." ... [Kissinger's Washington attorney] Lloyd Cutler [a counsel for both Presidents Carter and Clinton] wrote us: "In the light of his well-deserved reputation as a scholar and his considerable accomplishments as a public servant, I would think it is outrageous to suggest that his published writings are designed to line his pockets rather than to advocate policies that he believes will best serve the public interest."[2]

In the same program's final segment, "H. Ross Perot," Morley Safer explored the intriguing Perot for President movement, which elicited Perot's comment about the federal deficit, "It's like a crazy aunt you keep down in the basement. All the neighbors know she's there, but nobody talks about her." Safer, besides detailing Perot's business background, interviewed volunteers in the Perot Independent movement. Safer said of the Texas populist:

Perot's message is not a whole lot different from other men who've bashed away at a populist theme. . . . And what Americans love most of all is a maverick, an untamed cowpoke willing to ride in and clean up the town, especially one who's willing to blow $100 million to get hired for a job he says he really didn't want.[3]

Perot announced several months later that he would not be a candidate, but his name was still put on the ballot in all fifty states and he remained a factor in the closely contested presidential election in 1992, especially after he announced in the early fall that he was re-entering the race. His vote amounted to approximately 19 percent of the total in November 1992, the best showing of a third candidate since Theodore Roosevelt came in second in 1912 when running against Governor Woodrow Wilson of New Jersey and President William Howard Taft.

NOTES

1. The difficulty for American correspondents covering Hussein was exemplified by Australian-born American citizen Peter Arnett of CNN who was attacked by conservative senators. For details, see Peter Arnett, *Live from the Battlefield* (New York: Simon & Schuster, 1994).

2. Transcript: CBS News, "60 Minutes" XXIV, no. 28 (March 29, 1992).

3. Transcript: CBS News, "60 Minutes" XXIV, no. 28 (March 29, 1992).

Chapter Five

Beginnings and Development of the "48 Hours" Series

The CBS News division, seeking to build on the success of "60 Minutes," during the 1980s introduced the weekly program (except for special event cancellations) entitled "48 Hours" with Dan Rather in the moderator's role which Mike Wallace so successfully handled in the development of "60 Minutes."

Rather served as moderator in addition to his role (begun in 1981) as CBS Evening News anchor (a position he began to share with Connie Chung in 1993).

In January 1988 the "48 Hours" program began its successful run. An early program—Program No. 5, in fact—dealt with the presidential campaign. Entitled "In the Campaign," it covered events in the New Hampshire primary campaign using the "soft news" approach.

Participants in the early presentations of "48 Hours" included Dan Rather (moderator), Lesley Stahl, Bill Plante, Bruce Morton and Bob Faw. All have had considerable experience with CBS News, unlike some of the participants in "West 57th," another show which was experimented with and later dropped from the schedule after a couple of years with some degree of success. The latter show was aimed at younger viewers; the "48 Hours" audience demographics seemed to indicate it was aimed at the broader general public.

Dan Rather introduced the program with a discussion of the relative standings of the 1988 presidential candidates. On the

Republican side, candidates were Vice President George Bush, Senator Bob Dole (R-Kansas), former Delaware Governor Pierre DuPont, Congressman Jack Kemp (R-New York), and the Reverend Pat Robertson (son of a Virginia U.S. Senator, the late A. Willis Robertson), the right-wing television evangelist.

On the Democratic side, candidates were Governor Michael Dukakis of Massachusetts, U.S. House of Representatives floor leader Representative Richard Gephardt of Missouri, the Reverend Jesse Jackson, Senator Paul Simon of Illinois, Senator Albert Gore, Jr., of Tennessee, Governor Bruce Babbitt of Arizona, and Senator Gary Hart of Colorado (who withdrew under a cloud early in the campaign).

Interviews were done in the first caucus state, Iowa, by correspondents who sought to provide background on individual candidates as well as voters' views. A module, "Back of the Pack: Monday 5:49 a.m.," found Lesley Stahl quizzing Arizona Governor Bruce Babbitt, who stated that despite a less than overwhelming showing in Iowa, he planned to take his campaign on to New Hampshire. At the time, the Iowa caucuses showed Gephardt and Simon doing well in Iowa, but Dukakis was expected to run well and perhaps win in New Hampshire, his neighboring state.

BORDER PATROL AND GAMBLING FEVER

On January 8, 1992, "48 Hours" dealt with "Desperate Journey," a feature on the Border Patrol. Unlike "60 Minutes," which normally has three segments on different topics, "48 Hours" has several segments, but they are all on related topics which are part of an overall subject. Dan Rather's introduction explained why so many individuals try to cross the Mexican-U.S. border illegally. In the first module, "Border War," Bernard Goldberg investigated skirmishes along the border between would-be illegal immigrants and the Border Patrol. Phil Jones, correspondent for "Labor Pains," interviewed Mexican and Central American workers in a camp at Encinitas, California, near the border.

Harold Dow, in "Paper Chase," termed Los Angeles "the mecca for new immigrants." Immigration and Naturalization Service (INS) agents discussed their activities with new immigrants. How undocumented workers falsify papers was a focus. It was detailed and specific. In "Killing Fields," Phil Jones examined Long Beach, California, and its immigrants. One of these was Chum Nhek, forty-five, who was shot at by a Mexican-American street gang in Long Beach. In "Charge of the Night Brigade," Bernard Goldberg interviewed several illegal immigrants and INS agents. Harold Dow, in "Fatal Impact," discussed a homicide charged to two Korean immigrants, Soon Ja Du and Latasha Harlins. In the homicide a Korean-American store worker was shot by a woman who had been accused of stealing merchandise. In "Final Journey," Goldberg told how Cuban refugees tried to flee into Florida and told of Gregorio Perez, who died while attempting to reach the Florida coast by raft. This segment also dealt with Haitian refugees seeking sanctuary in Florida.

This enlightening program brought to its audience useful information about the growing problem of illegal immigrants in the United States; it showed personal facets of their lives while in danger of discovery.

In "Gambling Fever," aired January 15, 1992, Dan Rather focused on the start of legal gambling in some areas of the United States. In "You Bet Your Life," CBS correspondent Erin Moriarty interviewed Jim Howard, a compulsive gambler in federal prison, and his wife, Julia, who told of their experience with the compulsive gambling habit. The gambler in question staged a kidnapping, resulting in his conviction and imprisonment, when his wife wanted to buy a house with money he had lost at gambling.

Correspondent Bernard Goldberg in "All That Glitters" investigated gambling in South Dakota's Black Hills. He interviewed the casino manager of the Midnight Star in Deadwood, South Dakota.

Scott Pelley in "Bingo" interviewed a bingo hall worker in Pittsburgh, who took riders on a bus tour to gambling resorts, including a Cherokee Indian reservation in North Carolina. Dan Rather also spoke with a gambler at the Alton Belle Riverboat Casino tied up at Alton, Illinois.

In "A Day at the Races," Richard Schlesinger went to Maryland's Worrell Track to interview racing gamblers. One woman told of paying income tax on $250,000 of gambling winnings. In the segment "Long Way Home," Erin Moriarty interviewed a gambler named Lorraine in Billings, Montana, after video gambling became legal there. She also interviewed counselors who work with compulsive gamblers to help them to give up the gaming habit.

In "Low Roller," Bernard Goldberg conducted additional interviews in Deadwood, South Dakota, with members of Gamblers Anonymous.

This "48 Hours" program gave some useful insights into a social problem which resulted from the legalization of gambling, which had resulted from the need of various states and local jurisdictions to raise money to balance their budgets. It also showed how this impacted related social problems, which had to be dealt with in the political system.

LONELY HEARTS SWINDLES, PRIZE SHOWS AND ASSASSINS

Court cases growing out of "lonely hearts" swindles made up the subject of the "48 Hours" program for January 22, 1992, "For Love or Money," introduced by Dan Rather. Rather's own interview dealt with the phenomenon of deprogramming by families of those who have been brainwashed by religious fanatics or others.

Phil Jones, CBS correspondent, in "My Brother's Keeper—Part One," interviewed Frank Scott of Bellingham, Washington, who was engaged in a court battle with his brother, Rex, regarding who was responsible for taking care of Rex. Joe Roberts, who had Rex's power of attorney, was involved in the case. Judge David Nichols said if money weren't involved in the case, it wouldn't have come into court. Erin Moriarty in a segment "Test of Strength," interviewed Lucille Ashcraft, the object of another controversy about an elderly person's care.

The program's discussion threw light on the tangled problems involved in legal guardianships and indicated how this is becoming a more important social and political problem as an increasing number of citizens enter the more advanced age categories.

On January 26, 1992, the "48 Hours" program, "Get Rich Quick," told how some people can become millionaires and others try to do so through scams which represent ways to get quick money. In "Only in America," Bernard Goldberg interviewed Tom Vu, operator of a seminar teaching how to make millions in real estate. Some of those in his real estate seminar called it a scam, but the operator said it was a legitimate business.

In "Dialing for Dollars—Part One," Phil Jones interviewed Tom Sedivy, who participates in radio contests and has won $200,000 worth of prizes and cash, including a new Corvette and twenty trips to Hawaii. Richard Schlesinger in another segment, "For Love or Money," interviewed Genie Polo Sayles, who said her business is making a study of rich men. In "Dialing for Dollars—Part Two,"

Phil Jones went further into the story of Tom Sedivy, "radio contest king," with other accounts of his winning efforts in contests.

Erin Moriarty in "Lucky Day' interviewed the host of "Hoosier Millionaire," a television show awarding prizes and based in Indianapolis. Moriarty noted how some contestants stop short of the maximum $1 million prize on the show.

In concluding, Dan Rather noted that these individuals will continue to compete as long as the prizes are there.

The occasional charges that scams are being operated provoke action in the courts from time to time, but this program investigated a significant issue for persons who follow games and contests.

On the February 5, 1992, "48 Hours," in the segment "JFK," which was later issued on video after the Oliver Stone movie, Dan Rather discussed the Kennedy assassination of 1963 and the many ensuing investigations (Rather was present in Dallas on November 22, 1963). Persons referred to included Jim Garrison, Richard Helms of the CIA, history professor Michael Kurtz at Southeast Louisiana University, Mark Lane, who wrote *Rush to Judgment,* and investigative reporter Jonathan Kwitny. The Rather segment, which incorporated the much replayed Zapruder assassination film, involved interviews with witnesses at the scene and others involved in the various investigations. In "Mystery Man" Phil Jones discussed the strange life of Lee Harvey Oswald, accused of killing President Kennedy but never tried because he himself was slain by Jack Ruby two days after the President's death. Some footage of a reporter's interview with Oswald shortly before his death was presented. In another segment, "Suspects," Richard Schlesinger discussed the eyewitness account of deaf mute Ed Hoffman and the theory of history professor Michael Kurtz, who believes Kennedy had ordered the murder of Fidel Castro but Castro was successful in ordering Kennedy's murder before he himself was made a target. Other discussion revolved around Carlos Marcello, the reputed boss at the time of the New Orleans mob. In a final segment, "Scenario," Dan Rather interviewed Kevin Costner, who played Jim Garrison in the movie *JFK,* and Oliver Stone, producer of the film. Rather noted that the House investigation of the Kennedy assassination may be fully reported if those files are opened. They were scheduled to be kept closed until the year 2029, but many were opened in 1993 as a result of new congressional legislation. Rather concluded, "Just as we cannot know where John Kennedy would have led us in life, so we may never know enough to answer all questions about his death."

Although this program did not introduce much that was new about the assassination, it did provide valuable context and updated the available information. It was a useful report.

In the February 26, 1992, "48 Hours" report, "On Hate Street," Dan Rather focused on the killing of Yusef Hawkins, who was the victim of an apparent racial attack in New York. In "Rising Star," Phil Jones dealt with Michael Lowe, Grand Dragon of the Knights of the Ku Klux Klan. Richard Schlesinger in "Hatebusters" dealt with gay activists in Boston who seek to help solve hate crimes against gay men. Erin Moriarty in "Noisemaker" dealt with the activities of the Reverend Al Sharpton in New York, who involved himself in the Yusef Hawkins case. In "Show Time" Phil Jones investigated how the work of the Ku Klux Klan was being pursued in Denver, where African American citizens staged a counter-march to that of the Klan. In "Atrocity," CBS correspondent Rita Braver investigated activities at Ohio State University, where Holocaust "revisionist" Bradley Smith tried to claim that the Nazi Holocaust was a hoax. Rabbi Steve Abrams stated that Smith's work was an effort to stir up anti-Semitism. In "Showdown," CBS News correspondent Ron Allen investigated the work of the Oregon Citizens Alliance, which opposed gays and lesbians in pursuit of its agenda of family values. In "Class Struggle" Erin Moriarty developed the story of New Utrecht High School in Brooklyn, New York, where many ethnic groups contribute students to the school's enrollment list. Dan Rather concluded the broadcast by observing that "on Hate Street, the wounds heal slowly and the scars last forever."

The program added to public knowledge about hate crimes and how religious, ethnic and racial prejudice add to the social and political problems of the American polity. It was thus a valuable contribution to the understanding of basic social problems, following in the tradition of other significant topics covered on "48 Hours" as well as "60 Minutes." Some defenders of the status quo might attack this approach as being "politically correct," but it clearly dealt with an important political and social issue and added to the potential for public insight into these issues.

The "48 Hours" format has been ingeniously used by CBS News. It has provided a pattern which other networks have tended to follow in constructing their magazine programs, and as the genre has grown it has become second only to "60 Minutes" (and perhaps ABC's "20/20") in setting a pattern for successful electronic magazine programs.

STALKERS, POACHERS, UNEMPLOYMENT
AND MURDER VICTIMS

The "48 Hours" for March 4, 1992, "Stalker," featured Dan Rather, Richard Schlesinger, Phil Jones and Erin Moriarty. The opening segment, "Stalker," dealt with the obsession of Robert Bardo with a young television actress, Rebecca Schaeffer, whom he killed after stalking her. She was one of the stars of the show "My Sister Sam."

Dan Rather said one stalking victim called stalking "a never-ending hell." A segment with correspondent Phil Jones, "Fatal Obsession," dealt with details of Bardo's obsession with Rebecca Schaeffer. Dr. John Stalberg, a psychiatrist, described Bardo as "one of the sicker people I've seen."

Gavin Debecker, a Hollywood security expert, said he felt the biggest mistake was made when the actress responded to a fan letter from Bardo, who was a stranger to her. When he rang the doorbell, she answered her apartment door, and that was the moment at which he killed her. Arrested at his Tucson home, he was later convicted of first-degree murder.

In another segment, "Fan Mail," Erin Moriarty spoke about the man who stalked actress Andrea Evans of "One Life to Live." This problem continued for five and a half years. Her stalker slashed his wrists. She finally moved to a new and secret address. FBI Special Agent Jim Wright was interviewed about this same case. The FBI charged the stalker with sending threats through the mail and he switched to a private delivery service.

In Richard Schlesinger's segment, "Stranger," the correspondent interviewed Arthur Navarro, a man stalked by a woman admirer. Navarro finally got a restraining order to keep her away from him. Police Chief Darryl Gates of Los Angeles told Schlesinger such stalking cases had to be taken seriously.

Erin Moriarty in "House Calls" described how a mystery woman had been stalking Jim Barr for six months. Barr was a family doctor with a practice near Columbus, Ohio. Erin Moriarty even interviewed Dr. Barr's wife, Martha.

Richard Schlesinger's segment "Starry Eyes" dealt with people who attend special events with knives and guns. He talked with security officers and psychiatrists about this problem. These included Bruce Danto, a psychiatrist who worked with West Coast detectives.

In "Fatal Obsession," Phil Jones showed the sentencing of Robert Bardo, the murderer of Rebecca Schaeffer. He interviewed her parents and Bardo's attorney, Steven Galindo.

Dan Rather closed the program with the news that Dr. Jim Barr now believes he has determined the identity of the mystery woman who has been following him.

This "48 Hours" exposed the fact that the behavior of these stalkers is not merely a nuisance but a threat to their would-be victims. It helped the public to have a better understanding of this problem and thus contributed to public enlightenment. Some might charge that this information is sensational, but it clearly contributes to crime prevention.

The March 18, 1992, "48 Hours," entitled "Hard Times Hit Home," was moderated by Dan Rather. In "Hanging Tough," unemployed people were interviewed. Dan Rather noted that "everyone . . . now acknowledges that the recession is a serious national problem."

Phil Jones' "American Nightmare" focused on job hunters who were having little success. Jones described their former jobs and their current efforts to secure new employment.

In "Close to Home," Richard Schlesinger described how one thousand people crowded into a New Jersey ballroom seeking to buy homes repossessed by the Resolution Trust Corporation (RTC) after the lending institutions had lost their charters. Their difficulties in this situation were explored with interviewees whose incomes were more limited than in the past.

In "Chain Reaction," Phil Jones studied unemployment and the recession in Stratford, Connecticut. He discussed with interviewees the work of a local bankruptcy attorney.

In Erin Moriarty's "Dream Girl," the correspondent examined how Cathy Meridig was trying in mid-recession to start a new business, selling toys that help build a young girl's self-esteem.

Giselle Fernandez, in "Hard Lesson," examined a little girl's birthday party in Ware, Massachusetts. In that city the fourth grade was being taught in the same building as the jail and courthouse. A building inspector had ordered the building closed.

Richard Schlesinger in "Close to Home" covered an auction of foreclosed homes and condos then owned by the federal government. He interviewed an auctioneer and bidders and observed the process.

Erin Moriarty, in "Starting Over," interviewed Maryann and Tom Petrowski, a couple who had been forced by the recession to move to a new location. After a move to Florida, their hard times had lingered.

Dan Rather concluded the roundup with a brief discussion of the Hansen family, who had moved into a new apartment and disclosed that Bob Hansen "finally got a job as a warehouse foreman."

This program—which could be called a "backgrounder"—gave good insights into the plight of middle-class unemployed people who suffered from the recession in the dislocation of their careers and in other ways.

On the next program, the topic shifted from the economy to crime. On March 25, 1992, "48 Hours" covered the shocking crime of the killing of three girls at a yogurt stand in Austin, Texas. After an introduction by Dan Rather, Erin Moriarty, in "The Murders," described how Jennifer and Sarah Suraci and Amy Ayers were attacked and killed.

Phil Jones, in "Homicide Squad," interviewed friends of the three murder victims. All found the slayings hard to accept and even to believe.

James Hattori, in "Missing," interviewed families of the victims of other crimes, including Lori Bible, whose sister was abducted. Another crime investigated was the disappearance of Colleen Reed.

In "Afraid," Erin Moriarty interviewed an instructor at a shooting range in the Austin area. They discussed how fear follows in the path of violent crime. Instructor Diane Lawson told of efforts to train people to defend themselves.

Erin Moriarty, in "Suspects," interviewed members of the Austin homicide task force in the police department. Phil Jones, in "Homicide," discussed Austin's third murder of the year and the ensuing investigation.

In "Hunted" James Hattori interviewed Detective Bruce Boardman about the then-unsolved murder case of Harold Carter of Austin. Another victim whose family was interviewed was Cerelle Belt.

In "Homicide Squad," Phil Jones investigated a murder case in which Austin police were interrogating a subject.

In "We Will Not Forget," Phil Jones interviewed the Suraci family about the song "We Will Not Forget," written in memory of the murder victims.

Dan Rather concluded that "the families are still having good days mixed with bad." Other suspects had been investigated and cleared and that was where things stood at the time the broadcast was aired.

This broadcast was feature material with human interest aspects, but it could be categorized as part of the criminal justice aspect of the coverage. It examined one symptom of a nationwide trend toward more widespread commission of felonies.

On April 1, 1992, the broadcast topic, "Treasure Hunt," was not specifically political, although legal aspects of the ocean salvaging industry were discussed.

On April 15, 1992, on "48 Hours" Dan Rather introduced a program entitled "Family Secret," in which he noted that fifty thousand Americans are adopted each year and observed that in some cases they may not wish to know all the details of how they were adopted.

In "The Arrangement," Erin Moriarty looked into the case of Dana, a woman expecting a new baby, and interviewed her and her family. This mother had previously given up one child for adoption.

Harold Dow in "The Search" told the story of a twenty-seven-year-old New Yorker, Fred Ingram, who was obsessed with finding his natural mother. He was still looking at the time of the interview.

In "The Visitor" Edie Magnus interviewed Bill Pierce of the National Committee for Adoption. They discussed another adoption case and the principals involved.

Richard Schlesinger in "Lost and Found" told about the case of Sheri Wells, born in a Louisiana home for unwed mothers. At eighteen, she had registered with the National Reunion Network and was in the process of seeking her natural mother.

In the same April 15, 1992, "48 Hours," Erin Moriarty in the segment "The Choice" interviewed Linda Nunez, who is considered a "matchmaker" for adoptive children and their natural parents. She also interviewed two of Nunez's clients, Christina and Sandra. This was an enlightening module with an informational quality.

In "Lost and Found: Day Two," Richard Schlesinger interviewed reunited mothers and their children. He learned of one who had been through an eighteen-year wait. One of the natural daughters was the only child the mother ever had. He discussed with these people some of their emotional reunions.

Erin Moriarty in "Giving Up Baby" discussed the relationship between adoptive parents and natural parents when there is a dispute over custody of children. She interviewed two such couples at the Hospital of the Good Samaritan in an undisclosed city.

Dan Rather in the final wrapup of the program discussed a son and a daughter reunited with their respective natural parents.

This was an excellent human interest program, which—while covering some of the same kind of material discussed in tabloid programming—gave great insights into the feelings of the persons involved in these reunions as well as those adoptive and natural parents whose interests had come into conflict. This is a very good example of the emotive as opposed to factual impact of the so-called new journalism—ratings driven but not necessarily always totally so. The fact that this seems to be the case perhaps represents the presence in the broadcast spectrum of public broadcasting channels. Commercial programming can be affected by these as well as by tabloid programming such as "Hard Copy" and its ilk.

HEROIN CONNECTION, FAST BUCK SCAMS AND FORENSICS

On April 22, 1992, Dan Rather and "48 Hours" correspondents devoted their hour to "The Heroin Connection." The program examined policing of heroin and other drug smuggling by the Drug Enforcement Administration (DEA) and Rather was joined by Phil Jones and Richard Schlesinger in the program.

Rather spoke in the introduction of "a new threat from an old enemy: heroin." Smugglers included Chinese, Russians and even Colombians, according to Rather.

In a module entitled "Hide and Seek" with sights of Bangkok, Richard Schlesinger interviewed DEA agent Bruce Barnes, who works for his agency at the Bangkok airport. Schlesinger also interviewed Glen Cooper, another DEA agent in Bangkok, who is in charge of the DEA office there. Each told of his experiences with smugglers.

In another module, "Raw Recruits," Bernard Goldberg spoke of work done in Dallas by DEA agents, who work to oppose smugglers who take drugs into Texas from such places as Nigeria and Asia. Referring to the "Dallas connection," Goldberg spoke with DEA agents Tony Rust and Marty Kroft, as well as other agents, discussing smuggling techniques used by those smuggling drugs into Dallas. Goldberg also interviewed DEA agent Tim Silver of Dallas.

Erin Moriarty in the module "Sidewalk Sale" discussed drug dealing in New York City with John Galia, an undercover detective looking for drug dealers in New York. A man named Jake in East Harlem was also interviewed. Ms. Moriarty interviewed Jerry Winthrop, an undercover agent, and DEA agent John Dow, as well as an unidentified lab technician. Each spoke about cocaine being replaced by crack and other substances in New York.

Dan Rather in "Consumer Reports" interviewed recovering addicts Jason, Sandra and Chris about their experiences with heroin. He also interviewed Dr. Lorraine Hendricks, Regent Hospital adolescent drug treatment program officer, who spoke of the twelve- to twenty-one-year-old users with whom she deals.

Phil Jones in "Opium Country" interviewed the agents in the Burmese poppy fields in which some opium and other drugs originate. Phil Jones rode a donkey into the jungle in Burma in order to interview General Khun Sa, known in Burma as the "king of opium"; later he interviewed Brooklyn prosecutor Kathy Palmer, who is on the trail of Khun Sa, under indictment for drug smuggling. Jones also interviewed Tsang Joi, a foreign affairs official in the Shan army, as well as unidentified poppy growers in Burma.

In "War Story," another module, Lieutenant John Gallo was interviewed by correspondent Randall Pinkston, who examined drugs in North Philadelphia and who also interviewed District Attorney Lynn Abraham and Helen Anthony, whose home in Philadelphia was confiscated by DEA agents in the war against drugs.

In "Dead End," Richard Schlesinger provided further information about Bangkok, where he discussed how drug smugglers are dealt with by the law, as there is a death penalty or a twenty-five-year prison term. He also interviewed two women, Rachel and Velma, who were prosecuted for smuggling heroin in Bangkok. DEA Agent Bruce Barnes also spoke about the two women, who turned up in New York.

In the conclusion Dan Rather, on the "48 Hours" set, wrapped up the program by asking how serious a threat the new heroin connection is. He said that it is possible that "a new epidemic is under way," according to government sources.

This program was informative, but more than that it was informative about a major social program, just as Rather's famous program "48 Hours on Crack Street" and its sequel "Return to Crack Street" were.

On May 13, 1992, Dan Rather introduced the special "48 Hours" program entitled "Hard Evidence," which dealt with investigations in murder cases by forensic experts. Rather interviewed Bill Fleyscher, a commissioner of the Vidocq Society, who described a case in which evidence experts proved that a woman's death was a murder, not a suicide. Detective Jerry Giorgio of the New York

City police told of a little baby girl whose body was found beside a highway and triggered a search for her killers.

In the segment "Baby Hope" Rather interviewed police who started a 1991 inquiry in the shadow of the George Washington Bridge in New York City. It was there that police found a beverage cooler containing a human body. Detective Joe Neenan of the New York City police said the body was found in a plastic bag. Rather noted that it was "the decomposed body of a child, a malnourished little girl." Neenan found the girl was four to five years old and Detective Jerry Giorgio said New York police called her "Baby Hope" because they hoped that someone would identify her someday and help find those responsible for her death.

Rather also interviewed a psychic, Dorothy Allison; FBI forensic lab specialist Eugene O'Donnell; and Smithsonian Institution anthropologist Douglas Ubelaker, who joined the investigation.

Richard Schlesinger in "Mystery on the Menu" interviewed Commissioner Bill Fleyscher of the Vidocq Society, whose quarterly meeting was being held in the Old City Tavern in Philadelphia and which was investigating the Heidi Berg murder, which occurred in August 1991 when the twenty-seven-year-old woman vanished. Her skeleton was found several months later in a gravel pit; police had earlier failed to find her body.

Fleyscher discussed details of the case with Schlesinger in this segment, in which he described how the Vidocq Society was named after Eugene Francis Vidocq, who in 1813 formed the French Sûreté, the first detective organization in the world. They discussed another case triggered by a disappearance and other murder cases looked into by society members.

In another module, "Scene of the Crime," Rita Braver of CBS interviewed Jason Alexander, who compiled data on a computer; Luke Haag, an expert on crime scene reconstruction; and Michael Kennedy, lawyer for Jim Mitchell, whose brother Artie was killed and who was accused in the crime. Details of this case were discussed, and in the next segment, "Expert Witness," Erin Moriarty delved further into it with Dr. Louise Robbins of the University of North Carolina at Greensboro. She dealt with foot and shoe print evidence, which became controversial when she took this evidence into the courtroom and it went beyond an academic exercise. Erin Moriarty also interviewed FBI special agent William Bodziak about the case and referred to the case of Stephen Buckley, dealt with in a later module.

In "Dead Reckoning," Phil Jones discussed the death of a forty-three-year-old man who was killed because he was dating a twelve-year-old girl. Dr. William Bass, an anthropologist, told of testifying in court about the murder, on which the Tennessee anthropologist and his students had worked to reconstruct details.

A further interview with Fleyscher was conducted by Schlesinger in "Mystery on the Menu," which dealt with the murder of Zoia Assur. Schlesinger interviewed a lie detector expert, Nate Gordon, as well as others involved in this case. Dan Rather raised the question whether in this case a footprint used in court might have sent an innocent man to prison as the slayer.

In "Rare Medium" Doug Tunnell interviewed Police Detective Ralph Pauldine about a South Florida murder case in which the victim, Leo Beauregard, was stabbed to death. Detectives described the development of their case. Tunnell asked whether a psychic like Noreen Reneir can help the police solve such a crime. He then spoke of a double killing which occurred in Colonie, New York, and is still being investigated.

Erin Moriarty joined Tunnell in looking into the story of murder suspect Stephen Buckley and interviewed prosecutor Tom Knight. Other investigators also told their views of the case.

In "Hearing Is Believing" Phil Jones told the story of a teenage boy considered brain dead after a highway accident. Details of this case were probed. A damage suit was involved in this matter.

Hattie Kauffman in "Burning Questions" looked into a Los Angeles case in which a fire was believed to have been fatal to an elderly woman. The case, still being investigated, was the object of an arson investigation in Los Angeles after the 1992 riots.

In "Grave Doubts" Richard Schlesinger interviewed Dr. James Starrs of George Washington University about a hatchet murder case. Dr. Starrs, who specializes in old crimes, was asked about the Lizzie Borden case. Lizzie Borden was accused of murdering her parents in a widely discussed event in the nineteenth century. Dr. Starrs also conducted an investigation into the assassination of Senator Huey Long in Louisiana in 1935. He visited the crime scene in the Louisiana State Capitol with Schlesinger.

In a further module, "Expert Witness," Erin Moriarty investigated a case that occurred in Logan, Ohio, in 1982, in which a young couple disappeared and their dismembered bodies were later found in a cornfield. The sentencing by a three-judge panel of the girl's stepfather, Dale Johnston, was described. The convicted man received the death penalty, and the evidence that convicted him was discussed. The appeal that eventually lifted the death sentence was described, and he was released from death row in 1990. Another murder case was also discussed in this segment.

In "Mystery on the Menu—Part Three" Schlesinger conducted a final interview with Bill Fleyscher in which they discussed the murder case of Zoia Assur. Schlesinger also interviewed Detective James Churchill, who worked on the case, which had still not been brought to a conclusion at airtime.

Dan Rather closed the broadcast by noting advancements made in the science of crime detection. This program used to considerable advantage the approach of focusing in depth on a single subject. It was an educational program which revealed much about new developments in the science of forensic technology. It did not simply use sensational approaches as the tabloid programs do but went into detail about new developments and contributed to public knowledge. It was in the CBS tradition and came as near as commercial programming ever does to the standard usually set by public television.

The May 20, 1992, "48 Hours," entitled "Pet Passion," had no political content.

Another interesting program was aired on January 20, 1993, when Dan Rather presented an interview done during the pre-inauguration period with newly elected President Bill Clinton.

The next chapter will deal with "Street Stories," a now-defunct program narrated by Ed Bradley, also of "60 Minutes."

Chapter Six

"Street Stories" Program Content in 1992 and 1993

By 1993 the "Street Stories" series, moderated by Ed Bradley on CBS and begun several years earlier, was one of a welter of magazine programs which included CBS' "60 Minutes" as well as "48 Hours" (CBS), "20/20" and "PrimeTime Live" (ABC), "Dateline NBC" and two 1993 newcomers, "Now with Tom and Katie" (NBC) and "Day One" with Forrest Sawyer (ABC), in addition to another recent addition, the Fox network's "Front Page."

Also on CNN there were such programs as "Crossfire," a debate show, and "Closeup," which may not be true magazine shows but are not quite straight news either. This listing excludes "Nightline" on ABC and the so-called tabloid shows. This variety indicates that the public had a much more voracious appetite for this type of programming in 1993 than it did when the genre began in the 1960s.

This continuing analysis deals with "Street Stories" aired late in 1992 and early in 1993, looking at those segments with political content.

The November 5, 1992, "Street Stories" began with a Bradley segment in which he was joined by Peter Van Sant interviewing individuals about their dealings with health maintenance organizations (HMOs). The timeliness of this was apparent since the health care crisis was reflected in numerous "60 Minutes" segments in the period previously analyzed. Bradley noted that Peter Van Sant's segment "tells us, because of the way that some HMOs are set up, some doctors may be making a fateful choice between saving lives and making money": hence the focus on medical ethics as well as public policy in this segment. Specific cases and interviews with medical doctors and patients were included in this module, which preceded by only a few months President Clinton's appointment of Hillary Rodham Clinton's Health Care Task Force.

The criminal justice theme found in earlier segments on other series appeared in a segment, "Family Ties," in which Farrell Gordon dealt with the dilemma of informing on his father, whom Jerry Bowen identified as a con artist. Material on the Gordon family background was included.

The last segment of the November 5, 1992, "Street Stories" dealt with an update of the Oregon Measure 9 proposal declaring homosexuality "abnormal, wrong, unnatural and perverse." It also covered AIDS-HIV controversies in dental offices in Massachusetts.

The success of these "Street Stories" was reflected by reports that in mid-1993 Bradley was negotiating with both CBS and ABC about future programs. He did stay with CBS.

On November 12, 1992, in its first segment, the program focused on a Veterans Day "peg" (timeliness factor) about a World War II atrocity: the Malmedy massacre of a large group of American soldiers during the Battle of the Bulge in 1944. Eyewitness interviews constituted the greater part of this Bob McKeown segment. The correspondent was one of those who covered the Persian Gulf War for CBS.

The Malmedy massacre was the object of congressional investigations in the 1950s, but McKeown's segment did introduce some new facts and provided some current interest.

The next segment on the November 12 program dealt with a civil action brought by Bob Kearns, inventor of the intermittent windshield wiper, against auto companies. At the time of the broadcast Kearns had won a judgment against the Ford Motor Company. The theme of this segment was basically that of scientific investigators against corporate America and the fallout from this kind of confrontation. The segment managed to deal with such human interest factors as the impact of the dispute on the inventor's marriage, a phenomenon noted in a PBS documentary on early electronic inventors such as Nikola Tesla which was aired prior to this broadcast.[1]

In a third segment presented by Harold Dow, "Red Blood," the focus was on the Colombo crime family, and once again the criminal justice system was the subject of investigation.

A final segment, "Home on the Range," dealt with Bradley's interview with women cattle herders and had no obvious political content.

On November 19, 1992, Bradley introduced Harold Dow's "Highway Robbery" segment, about the growing number of carjackings in urban America. Once again the criminal justice theme provided the program content. Interviews were made with police and victims as well as Kip Beasley, a convicted carjacker, who admitted to a drug addiction. Other details of the crime were noted and the news peg used was President George Bush's signing of legislation making carjacking a federal crime. The reporting had depth and provided context for the discussion of the growing problem.

Peter Van Sant narrated the next segment, "Trade Secrets," which dealt with espionage. General Viktor Budanov, formerly of the Soviet KGB, was the object of an investigation which dealt with efforts of former adversaries from Western intelligence agencies to collaborate on business ventures with former KGB men like General Budanov. Efforts of both sides to adjust to the new situation were a part of this coverage. The segment was effective in providing context and background.

In a Roberta Baskin segment, "Accident-Prone," the focus was on safety belts in cars, and the background was provided by victims of accidents as well as Joan Claybrook, former director of the National Highway Traffic Safety Administration. This gave useful background on the problem of regulatory aspects of highway safety.

In a final segment, "Son of a Gun," circus cannon performers were covered and the content was basically nonpolitical.

SOMALIA, HEALTH CARE POLICY, PRIVATE EYES AND TYLER, TEXAS

The "Street Stories" airing for December 10, 1992, was moderated by Ed Bradley; the first segment, "Restoring Hope," narrated by Bob McKeown, dealt with American military operations in Somalia. The segment described preliminary and initial operations seeking to restore some semblance of order to the African nation, which had been through a period of civil war and accompanying severe anarchy.

Interviews with International Medical Corps member Sam Toosey and patients and their families in Baidoa constituted human interest coverage of the early phases of the Somalian operation. The coverage was tentative but sought to present a "feel" for the situation developing there.

The second segment, "Mother's Intuition," explored another medical situation, the problems of a breast implant recipient interviewed by Rita Braver. This segment reflected the high degree of interest in the health care public policy area, as did magazine airings previously analyzed.

Rita Braver gave background and interviewed Jama Russano and pathologist Dr. Douglas Shanklin, discussing from a consumer point of view the problems of patients and physicians dealing with questionable implants, as well as a new group being formed by Mrs. Russano, Children Affected by Toxic Substance (CATS). This segment fell within the tradition of consumer exposé and was along the lines of the "Harvest of Shame" Murrow documentary of the 1960s although the emphasis was a little different. It was an effective piece of documentation.

In Harold Dow's December 10 segment on "Beating the Odds" Dow interviewed rap music entrepreneurs, a subject which did not contain overtly political content.

An economic theme which had potential political impact was dealt with in the segment "Detective Story," in which people working for service industries were interviewed. Operations of private eyes in the Los Angeles area were the focus of the piece, which included human interest factors. The item focused attention on an individual example of the problem of employment during a recession and thus dealt with a significant public policy theme.

On the December 12, 1992, "Street Stories," produced by Catherine Lasiewicz, Peter Van Sant probed into the problem of crime in a small town. In the "Tyler, Texas" segment, townspeople interviewed included an Episcopal priest, the Reverend Dr. David Gallaway. The inquiry was devoted to establishing the nature of small town life. A second interview, with the Reverend Daryl Bowdre, established the ethnic and racial boundary lines drawn in the town. This was by way of leading up to the racial and social problems generated by the fatal shooting of an eighty-four-year-old African American woman, Annie Rae Dixon. Van Sant interviewed the victim's daughter-in-law to learn the details of the slaying, which occurred at the hands of a white police officer from Kilgore, Texas. Through interviews Van Sant developed the story of the follow-up to the tragedy and the investigation which followed. In the process of developing this information an interview was done with Ku Klux Klan Grand Dragon Michael D. Lowe. Prospects of violence and discussion of ethics of the media in covering this potentially explosive series of events made up the remainder of the segment under analysis. The module ended with a discussion of prospects for racial harmony and the meager response to the Klan's attempt to hold a rally. No conclusion was stated to the piece; the technique used was that of marshaling facts and letting them speak for themselves.

In a segment which was the second presented in this airing, "Dental Hygiene Part I," the emphasis shifted from criminal justice to the public health care issue with focus on the AIDS epidemic. Bob McKeown investigated the danger arising to the public from improper handling of dental equipment. The story of AIDS victim Kimberly Bergalis of Florida was among those discussed.

The type of coverage presented in this segment has been criticized as media hyping of hysteria, but the news media argue that the watchdog role they play and the need to present such facts as a public service necessitate such coverage. It is indeed a controversy which involves public social psychology over this important issue.

In "Dental Hygiene Part II" McKeown continued his examination of the subject. He interviewed the following: Dr. Geraldine Morrow, president of the American Dental Association; Dr. Harold Jeffe, of the Centers for Disease Control in Atlanta; Drs. Martin Gottlieb and Robert Kolstad of the Baylor College of Dentistry; Drs. Rafael Santore and Gordon Christensen and infected victims Barbara Webb and Jim Sharpe.

An effort at fairness was made by presenting views of both victims and professionals. The discussion did not take a point of view as such, although it did point out that there is a shortage of sterilization equipment. Persons who become alarmed by exposés may argue that the information was unduly alarmist, but others believe that the segment was providing necessary public information. This is an unresolved issue, as it was for CBS.

In a final segment, "New World," Harry Smith investigated immigrants who encounter crime and modern social problems in New York City. Smith went to the Queens Adult Learning Center for his information about these problems of immigrants. His study dealt with a significant social problem and was informative. It could not be described as alarmist by any fair-minded critic, but it did present information significant to the public.

HEMOPHILIACS, HURRICANES AND
A MONTAGE FOR 1992

The December 17, 1992, "Street Stories," produced by Catherine Lasiewicz, dealt with the plight of hemophiliacs, a Croatian musician, and the aftermath of a hurricane.

The first segment, "Blood Feud," consisted of Richard Roth's look at hemophiliacs who had contracted AIDS. Roth conducted interviews at the Sierra Nevada Memorial Hospital with patients Tom Taylor and Loras Goedken, attorney Duncan Barr (representing Cutter Labs, a blood serum processor), and former Centers for Disease Control epidemiologist Dr. Donald Francis.

This portion of the problem presented a fair and balanced account of a public health problem, and it could be categorized as a public policy concern related to health matters. It could best be described as information without a specific viewpoint.

Political overtones could be found in the module "Knowing the Score," about a Croatian musician who was publicizing the plight of his people in the civil strife in the former Yugoslavia. Musician Nehad Bach was interviewed by Ed Bradley along with Bill Adler, a music industry publicist, and Danny Schechter of Global Vision (described by Bradley as "a television production company with an activist agenda").

This segment primarily presented a human interest view and did not present a political viewpoint but rather focused on how the artist represented his people.

In the segment "Broken Homes" Harold Dow interviewed victims of Hurricane Andrew along the Florida Gulf Coast and elsewhere. Victims discussed the havoc wrought by the hurricane and how it brought about difficult problems for the adoption system in Florida. This segment, more sociological than political, illustrated the problems encountered by local governments as a result of a major disaster like Hurricane Andrew.

A montage for year end was put together in "Street Stories 1992," the last segment presented by the group during the calendar year. Newsmakers covered in this final wrap-up section included first couple–elect Bill Clinton and Hillary Rodham Clinton, President George Bush, space shuttle crews, Olympic star Kristi Yamaguchi, L.A. riot beating victim Reginald Denny, a demonstrator who broke former President Reagan's crystal broadcasters award in Las Vegas, Bush's announcement about Somalia, an Amsterdam crash site, South African footage, and Mike Tyson on trial, as well as President Bush's collapse in Japan at a state dinner. Other subjects included Pope John Paul II, President Boris Yeltsin of the Russian Federation, an Elvis Presley stamp, earthquake damage, Princess Diana and Prince Charles, a fire, Johnny Carson, a tall ship, President Bush and Governor Clinton, as well as Pat Buchanan in campaign scenes. Further montage elements included Ross Perot, Paul Tsongas, Jerry Brown, Bob Kerrey, Tom Harkin, Bill Clinton, Vice President Dan Quayle, Al Gore, scenes from the presidential debates, Olympic stars, the Los Angeles police officers' trial in Simi Valley, California, state court, the Los Angeles riots and Rodney King and his mother. This segment was apparently a modern successor to the kind of news round table which used to be aired at the end of each calendar year, featuring correspondents from around the globe, in the radio era and in the early television era.

BACTERIOLOGICAL WARFARE, MARION BARRY AND KIDNAPPING

The "Street Stories" for January 7, 1993, focused on the issue of bacteriological warfare in a production by Catherine Lasiewicz. Other topics covered were the resurgence of tuberculosis and the attempted comeback of former mayor Marion Barry of Washington, D.C.

The presentation on germ warfare was in two segments; "Germ Warfare Part One" included correspondent Deborah Norville's interview with Glenn Holliman, a tuberculosis patient for whom doctors have been seeking a cure. Dr. Lee Reichman of the American Lung Association discussed causes of the tuberculosis resurgence. Norville also interviewed Jim McCormack, a commodities trader and TB patient. Others in the segment were Dr. James Cook of the National Jewish Center (NJC); Drs. Charles Peloquin and Leonid Helfets, also of NJC; Leonora Alston, an outreach worker; a patient named Michelle and others discussing this major public health problem.

In "Germ Warfare Part Two" Bradley introduced Norville, who traced the disease's history. She showed an inspection by Larrlidian Lindsay of the Fulton County Sheriff's Department and interviewed specialists in airborne diseases, including Drs. William Stead and Edward Nardell. Norville then summarized the problem.

In another module, "Talk of the Town," Jerry Bowen presented a case study of tuberculosis in Bath, Maine, and interviewed local citizens about it. In still another segment, "Chapter Two," Harold Dow delved into the comeback efforts of former D.C. mayor Marion Barry, who had returned home from a six-month prison term for a narcotics violation. The segment examined Barry's swearing in as a city councilman.

Finally, Ed Bradley updated the audience about several 1992 stories including those dealing with AIDS victim Gregory Scarpa, charged with two murders and himself a shooting victim, and Mark Nunez and Leo Bruce, jailed in connection with the murder of six Buddhist priests, who were both freed after a convict admitted the killings.

That concluded the program. Bradley and correspondents focused on a growing epidemiological problem in the United States, that of tuberculosis—once thought to have been eliminated. The updates of earlier stories continued in a tradition frequently followed on "60 Minutes."

"Street Stories" for February 25, 1993, included a part dealing with the search for a missing person ("Cat and Mouse") in which Richard Roth interviewed Detective Harold Sagan of the Fairfield, California, police department about the search for an apparent kidnapping victim, Amanda Campbell, that had continued in the area around San Francisco since 1983.

Amanda's mother, Ann Campbell, was interviewed along with Tim Binder, a suspect. The approach used in this story was one of human interest, and the story could be categorized as having a criminal justice theme.

In "Forging a Friendship," Deborah Norville probed into the relationship between two pen pals, one of them in prison. Their "lonely hearts" relationship ultimately turned out to be a fraudulent one. This provided a further example of consumer protection pieces, a continuing theme in the magazine series we have analyzed.

In "Off the Books," narrated by Rita Braver, correspondents looked into the "nanny" problem brought to the public's attention by the failed nomination of Zoe Baird to be Attorney General (ultimately Janet Reno of Florida was confirmed in the post). Rita Braver's interview showed how professionals are driven to break the law by the difficulty of finding suitable baby-sitters for their children.

Senator David Durenberger of Minnesota discussed the problem of these household workers. The segment gave useful background on a situation that apparently needed to be corrected to meet changing conditions. It did not specifically favor an updated amendment to the "nanny" law, but it did put the whole issue into context.

A Clark Gable segment, "The Boy Next Door," did not deal with a political topic.

On March 4, 1993, "Street Stories" discussed Dr. Jack Kevorkian, who has assisted suicides in various places. The first segment, however, dealt with sex offenders and convicted child molesters under the title "Not in My Neighborhood." This continued the criminal justice theme of various programs already analyzed.

In an additional story, "Overdrive," Roberta Baskin examined problems caused when truck drivers have accidents because of driving overly long hours. Several drivers were interviewed as well as Tom Koslowski of the Federal Highway Administration. The way in which log books are falsified, among other practices, was the topic of the remaining portion.

In a final segment, "Murder or Mercy," the case of Dr. Kevorkian was examined and the controversial physician was interviewed. Deborah Norville brought together various facts about the "mercy killing" practices involved in doctor-assisted suicides. Several cases were examined.

The remaining March 4 segment dealt with the skin problem of vitiligo experienced by entertainer Michael Jackson. Its content was basically non-political.

RELIGIOUS CULT, ABORTION PROTEST AND ALD TREATMENT

The "Street Stories" for March 11, 1993, with Ed Bradley as host and Catherine Lasiewicz as executive producer, included a segment dealing with the Waco, Texas, compound of David Koresh's Branch Davidian religious cult.

In the preceding segment correspondent Harold Dow presented "Lone Star Scandal," in which he interviewed the family of a murder victim killed by a parolee from a Texas prison, Allen McDuff. Dow visited a meeting of the Parents of Murdered Children support group in Houston. This was another criminal justice theme.

Dow's segment dealt with the controversy that surrounded former Texas Parole Board chairman Dr. James Granberry, an orthodontist. The segment was balanced and apparent fairness was achieved in presenting varying views of this controversy. It also had a human interest aspect and falls under the general category of criminal justice themes.

The second segment on the March 11 program, "Second Thoughts," was narrated by Deborah Norville, who interviewed a physician and an abortion protester about how it is possible to change one's position on the issue of abortions. Protesters were interviewed in the area around an abortion clinic where they were marching.

This discussion of the thorny abortion issue was handled in a sensitive and balanced manner.

In "How Much Hope" correspondent Peter Van Sant dealt with a case covered in the movie *Lorenzo's Oil*, the story of a Virginia couple who sought experimental treatment for their son, who had contracted the rare genetic disease adrenoleukodystrophy (ALD). The interviews dealt with the progress of another patient, a six-month-old boy who had been receiving the *Lorenzo's Oil* treatment for a year and a half. Van Sant also interviewed Augusto Odone, the father of the victim who was treated with the experimental compound.

This segment consisted primarily of human interest material but it discussed the health care issue, a recurring theme of magazine shows.

A final segment, "Being There," treated the Waco compound of David Koresh and the Branch Davidian sect, which became the notorious object of national attention when four Alcohol, Tobacco and Firearms (ATF) agents were killed in an attempted raid on the compound, which was later destroyed by the occupants, who set it aflame. Correspondent Bob McKeown interviewed a sect member who was not allowed to return to the compound after leaving. This sect member denied that the cult members would ever commit suicide, although all indications are that that is what occurred.

The April 1, 1993, "Street Stories" opened with the segment "Porn in the 'Hood," which dealt with controversy over a strip club in a residential neighborhood where the neighbors objected. Demonstrators and defenders of the business were both interviewed in an objective and balanced way.

In a second segment, "Fatal Practice," the interview by Peter Van Sant focused on the work of Dr. David Gunn, the abortion-performing gynecologist who was shot to death by an anti-abortion demonstrator in Florida. The segment focused on Dr. Gunn's background and early practice. The interviews also discussed the accused killer, who was later convicted, Michael Griffin. The module concluded with a discussion of how abortion doctors are arming themselves in self-defense.

In the segment "Plan of Attack" the story of the Waco Branch Davidian compound was updated. Bob McKeown interviewed an ATF agent who felt that the raid may not have been handled in the best possible way. Various aspects of the raid were discussed in a kind of postmortem.

A final module, "No Identifiable Reason," discussed the reaction of the public to mysterious diseases. The segment focused on a child in Morton Grove, Illinois, who had a disease caused by the victim's having had the AIDS virus. This provided background for a discussion of the AIDS epidemic, a major public health problem.

The April 8, 1993, "Street Stories" included a portion, "Dark Shadows," with interviews in a neighborhood of Los Angeles awaiting the second trial in the Rodney King case (the federal trial). But first the "Dark Shadows" segment dealt with the fixation of an adult man on a twelve-year-old girl, which caused him to become a stalker. Deborah Norville investigated this story and told how the offender went to prison. Another stalking victim and legislators considering laws to deal with the problem were also interviewed. The segment consisted mainly of exploring facts related to the problem.

In "Drawing the Line" the follow-up trial of the Los Angeles policemen involved in the Rodney King beating case was the focus of the segment. Bob McKeown went to Los Angeles' Koreatown to explore the apprehension of residents awaiting the follow-up trial.

In "Playing the Field" the focus was a basketball team, the Orlando Magic of Florida. The material was not political.

In the final segment "Lights! Cameras! Taxes!" Richard Roth explored difficulties taxpayers in the entertainment industry are having with a crackdown on lavish life-styles by the Internal Revenue Service (IRS). Roth interviewed both targets of the IRS investigation and agents involved in it. Part of the controversy hinged on the distinction between personal expenses and business expenses.

By 1993 the "Street Stories" series had ended. For a time there was a possibility that Bradley would leave CBS, although he did not. At this writing, he was still with CBS and appeared late in 1993 on a "60 Minutes" 25th anniversary program.

"Street Stories" had a fairly heavy emphasis on crime, but there was some human interest concern and it did explore several significant political issues. It had some resemblance to "60 Minutes" (particularly in format of in-depth interviews), but the focus seemed to be somewhat more on problems and issues and somewhat less on personalities than that of "60 Minutes," although it could still be described as sufficiently "soft" news to be considered magazine journalism.

NOTE

1. Tom Lewis, *Empire of the Air: The Men Who Made Radio* (companion volume to PBS documentary) (New York: Edward Burlingame/HarperCollins, 1991).

Chapter Seven

"West 57th" Contents

A relatively short-lived magazine program on CBS attracted attention during its brief span of a few years; it was aimed at a demographic group which had a core of younger viewers, according to most media critics. This program, "West 57th," developed some talent, correspondents who later appeared on more successful shows such as "60 Minutes." One correspondent, Meredith Vieira, had moved on to ABC's "Day One" at this writing.

This analysis will focus on selected programs in this series with a special emphasis on their political content.

The February 18, 1989, "West 57th" featured segments about Omar Sharif and about the AIDS epidemic. The portion which had the least political content was John Ferrugia's visit to the Columbus Zoo, a frothy piece which consisted of feature material. Ferrugia was joined by Karen Burns as narrator.

The program focused on the public health issue in a segment reported by Meredith Vieira and produced by Rob Hershman. The interviews concerned the death of AIDS victim Robert Steel. Two doctors presented different viewpoints about AIDS. Patients were interviewed, as well as Dr. Ken Fisher of Phoenix, Arizona. One interview module covered a patient being treated for lost vision, who had experienced some restoration of eyesight.

This was less significant than some other programs that covered the AIDS epidemic. It did not have much material dealing with the epidemic in general, but it did try to focus on human aspects of the disease, and it was true magazine coverage in that it dealt with human interest aspects of this growing social problem. This preceded by about four years the breakthrough mainstream film, *Philadelphia.*

The portion about the AIDS epidemic included interviews with the president of the American Foundation for AIDS Research and with a Yale Medical School professor who was critical of AIDS practice, as a kind of copout for physicians who did not want to deal with more difficult kinds of practice. This segment, although unremarkable, was an attempt to give a balanced portrayal of differing viewpoints. CBS correspondents working in this program included Meredith Vieira, Selina Scott, John Ferrugia and Karen Burns.

A final segment included material on someone who was only tangentially significant to current politics, Lawrence of Arabia. However, the thrust of the segment dealt less with the political aspects of Lawrence's career than with his portrayal in the remake of the movie *Lawrence of Arabia*, which featured Peter O'Toole. Omar Sharif, the star of the 1960s movie, and David Lean, the producer, were interviewed. Their discussion focused on cinematic production and techniques rather than on the political role played by Lawrence in the latter days of British colonialism in the Middle East. In timing, this discussion preceded the outbreak of the Gulf War, which had followed the Kuwait crisis in the summer of 1990, but the February 1989 production was presented at a time when there were growing tensions in the Middle East.

On the October 24, 1987, program, a political controversy about conservation of archaeological artifacts was covered in a Meredith Vieira segment; she interviewed the salvage team working on taking artifacts of the Spanish galleon *Atocha* from the Atlantic Ocean off the Florida coast. Archaeologist Duncan Acheson and his employer, a man named Fisher, were asked about their views of the galleon-salvage effort. Work done between 1973 and the date of the interviews was noted. Activities were outlined by the salvors and criticism of their work by environmental activists was included. Acheson defended the project as the work of para-archaeologists much as paralegal and paramedical work is done in other fields.

The segment continued with an interview with U.S. Representative Charles Bennett of Florida, who felt that the salvors were taking advantage of traditional admiralty law and expressed the view that the wreckage should be owned by the American public through the federal government and was sponsoring a bill to that effect.

The presentation dealt with the topic as a feature but it did mention the political controversy as part of the broader environmental issue. The issue's political aspects were discussed more incidentally as kind of an adjunct to the more feature-oriented summary done through interviews. Congressman Bennett claimed the work was too entrepreneurial and the salvor himself said some sites such as that of the *Titanic* should be off limits. Other views quoted indicated that salvors favored keeping such artifacts in the public domain except when their own work was concerned.

In general the Vieira interview was a workmanlike job but it maintained the demographic approach of the program.

Other program segments, "Cholesterol" and "Jah Love," were not primarily political. However, despite its feature aspects, a segment on *Rolling Stone*, the rock and roll magazine, which was celebrating its twentieth anniversary (1967–1987), narrated by Bob Sirrott, had political overtones. It described the magazine as a part of the "underground press" of the Vietnam era. Sirrott interviewed Jann S. Wenner, editor of the magazine, and examined coverage of such late 1960s events as the Woodstock music festival in upstate New York and a California "rock fest" of a similar nature which resulted in a riot. Participants' attention was mostly focused on the magazine's journalistic changes, but a reference to the identity of *Rolling Stone* as a periodical which covered both rock 'n' roll and revolution exhibited the political overtones. Writers such as Hunter S. Thompson and Tom Wolfe were interviewed, and headlines such as "Nixon Bites the Bomb" and a montage of magazine covers were also displayed.

The segment was pure nostalgia; while it did not focus on political content as a central theme, it did deal with the political issues of the times, particularly those of the founding period. Charges that it had sold out to the Establishment were also examined. The coverage was analytic to some extent, but like other material seen on "West 57th," it had some frothy elements.

COMMUNES, NAVY WHISTLE-BLOWER AND SECURITY REPORTING

The theme of criminal justice was developed in a "West 57th" October 31, 1987, segment narrated by Jane Wallace, entitled "Hare Krishna: Inside the Commune."

Jane Wallace, who later moved from CBS to her own syndicated program, asked commune members about child molestation charges made against them. She also probed into the slaying of Stephen Bryant and was told by Swami Bakhtapud (Keith Hahn, forty-nine), a Krishna leader, that there was a plot against Hare Krishna. The leader had founded Newbin Dobbin, which promoted transcendentalism, twenty years before in West Virginia. Since the commune's establishment various charges have been made against it. Wallace noted that most of the residents live below the poverty line and have donated money to construction of a palace of gold at the West Virginia site.

Wallace also delved into reports of Krishna undercurrents of violence, examining reports that skeletons of slain Krishna members had been dug up. Thomas Desher, a Krishna, was convicted of one murder and accused of another. He termed the murder charges and reports of sales of controlled substances a "concoction."

An effort was made to present the subject fairly by interviewing the accused, but the main thrust of the segment was that of an exposé. Current conditions in the compound are not known at this writing.

Meredith Vieira's segment on the Apollo Theatre in Harlem, "On Stage Dreams: At the Apollo," was not political and therefore will not be analyzed.

John Ferrugia presented a module entitled "Stephen Stockwitz: Presumed Guilty" about a Navy whistle-blower who accused contractors of breaking the law and was fired from his Naval Ocean Systems Center (NOSC) job in San Diego after an investigation by the Naval Investigation Service (NIS).

Stockwitz was described as an "excessive worker" who could be fired without cause. At the time of the interview he was fighting to clear his name of charges by legal counsel at the NOSC that he had violated several Navy regulations. Captain Patton, former commanding officer under whom Stockwitz worked, termed him a "keen minded professional," and the segment brought out that two promotions were given to Stockwitz during his time with the naval installation. On September 4, 1984, Stockwitz was accused by the NIS; at first he was told, "We can't tell you" what the charges were. Later he was informed that the charges included embezzlement of government funds and filing of a disputed travel claim. Stockwitz said the files showed that the charges were untrue and that NIS had talked to Captain Patton.

Stockwitz, who had attacked fraud and waste in government

contracts, considered his criticisms the real reason he was fired. A lieutenant commander was court martialed as a result of his investigation of fraud, and Stockwitz feels that an "old boy network" brought on his termination as a consequence. "I am determined to beat them for what they did," he told Ferrugia. He also said that a secretary, Kay Talley, spied on him and that his girlfriend, Angie Donawitz, said fifty-three love letters she had received were put into the investigative file. The woman charged that she felt "verbally and physically raped" by the investigation.

The Navy in San Diego and at the Pentagon refused to talk about the case. The NIS would not discuss its methods or its investigative ethics. Captain Patton said he was told nothing of the investigation. He termed it "an invasion of privacy, pure and simple." He said the NIS had approached a U.S. attorney to prosecute criminal charges against Stockwitz and was told twice that it had no case. The three and a half year battle of Stockwitz with the Navy had put him $20,000 in debt. He charged that the investigation would have a "chilling effect" on the Navy.

The segment was in the nature of an exposé; it was difficult to make it balanced because the Navy and the relevant subunit refused to discuss the case. This module indicates that military secrecy (however well-intentioned) complicates the task of the television journalist.

The armed forces apparently feel that government service is a privilege and that they bear a great responsibility in protecting the nation. Journalists are institutionally put at odds with this by the very nature of their task, and such conflicts are inevitable. During the 1980s two cases in progress in the courts reflected this institutional conflict. One involved Israeli commander General Ariel Sharon, who won a libel ruling but no damages against *Time* magazine. The other involved General William Westmoreland and CBS. This resulted in an out-of-court settlement involving an apology and no award of damages. Bystanders felt such court battles did little to enhance the stature of either litigant.

In general the CBS programs have been aggressive in digging up information and they have maintained journalistic standards of a high order, despite such incidents as that involving the so-called Benjamin Report made internally by a CBS executive. This case dealt with the production of a "CBS Reports" program, which resulted in a lawsuit involving Colonel Herbert and Mike Wallace. CBS was criticized in the broadcast profession and, unsurprisingly, in the print media, just as *Newsweek* in April 1994 criticized the whole genre of magazine programs.[1]

"West 57th" programs continued until 1989, but we have examined only a few select programs, preferring to concentrate on longer-lived series.

NOTE

1. Larry Reibstein, "The Battle of the TV News Magazine Shows: Trash + Class = Cash," *Newsweek* CXXIII, no. 15 (April 11, 1994): pp. 61–65. Also see Jonathan Alter, "Between the Lines: It Isn't All Junk Food: Believe It or Not, Prime-Time TV News Is More Informative Than Ever Before," *Newsweek* CXXIII, no. 15 (April 11, 1994): p. 66.

Chapter Eight

Aggressive Trends in Programming on ABC and NBC Magazines

This chapter will deal with networks that were historically late-comers to magazine programming but did have considerable competitive impact in the 1980s and 1990s. These networks are ABC and NBC. We will examine ABC first and will make only brief comments about NBC.

Alan Wurtzel, who in April 1994 was senior vice president for magazine programs for the ABC network, made the following comment about magazine programming:

"World News Tonight" is like the front section of the *Washington Post*. Magazine programs are like the Style section, Business, and the like. The issues are different and there is a different approach.

The lead time is a function of the structure of the broadcasts. On "World News Tonight" there is 24 hours. The magazine programs work on a weekly basis. Magazine programs have analogies to "the back of the book." They have different purposes.

The ABC executive also said that if one goes back and looks at the coverage of World War II and Korea, one can get a historical context for the Persian Gulf coverage. He said he wasn't in this position at that time, but historical analogies help. Edward R. Murrow did "Person to Person" at the same time he did "See It Now." We didn't call them magazine programs then, he noted, but one was "soft news" and one was "hard news."

WEEKLY APPROACH WITH LONGER SEGMENTS

Is there a difference? Yes, there's a difference in coverage, Wurtzel noted: In magazine shows, the issues are different; there are different players. Magazine programs generally are pre-planned and may take months to produce. No way does the same thing apply to "World News Tonight," he commented.

Segments are a different length in hard news. The genre is different; segments may run eight or nine to fifteen minutes on a magazine show; the sound bites may be one to two minutes, if that, on "World News Tonight."

There is more time to develop a feel for the characters in magazine narrative, he indicated. If you look at the way these are produced now and the way they were done in 1989 and 1990, you may see differences. These are based on different audience expectations.

Most of ABC's correspondents share Peter Jennings' strength as foreign correspondents. Forrest Sawyer was first into Kuwait, and Sheilah McVicker (also on "Day One") has the same kind of experience, according to Mr. Wurtzel.[1]

"20/20": A PIONEERING ABC PROGRAM

On ABC, the longest running magazine program has been "20/20," which was the predecessor of such later programs as "PrimeTime Live" and more recently "Day One," the latter begun in 1993.

The initial presentation of "20/20" was marked by low ratings when an Australian novice anchor team got bad reviews. It was after this occurrence that Downs and Walters were brought in and the program began to develop an audience.

Some of the early planning of ABC's programming was participated in by James C. Hagerty, who became an ABC vice president after leaving federal service as President Dwight D. Eisenhower's press secretary. His skills in program development are among the factors that have led over the years to the present popularity of ABC magazines.

Our principal attention in this chapter will be focused on the content of "20/20," which carries a good many psychologically oriented segments along with more purely political content. Sometimes these segments blend into political psychology; sometimes they do not and are pure human interest features without political content.

The major networks make efforts to be impartial in covering the news. But ABC's magazine programming tends to deal with a conservative (not necessarily Republican) agenda in contrast to CBS, which tends to have a liberal (not necessarily Democratic) agenda. Also topics on CBS tend to be more domestic, on ABC more international. Here we speak only of tendencies.

As for ABC's programming, we have sought to select political content over non-political content. Such segments as "Lennon's Kittens" are non-political, but portions like "Florida Hurricane Victims" have obvious political overtones.

In the earlier years of "20/20" a presidential candidate's negative publicity (Senator Gary Hart of Colorado, who later withdrew from the 1988 race) brought on an interview by Barbara Walters with Donna Rice, subject of a notorious photo with the senator on the boat *Monkey Business*. It of course had political impact but much of it was a personal inquiry into the background of Donna Rice.

A chronological survey of selected ABC programming, with "20/20" followed by "PrimeTime Live," follows:

On March 15, 1991, Barbara Walters conducted the first of several interviews with General Norman Schwarzkopf about his service in the Gulf War and his personal background. It was essentially a friendly interview; it reflected the considerable focus on Schwarzkopf as a war hero.

A widely publicized divorce was in the background of a May 24, 1991, "20/20" program. This interview preceded the divorce but the subject was Ivana Trump, the first wife of New York entrepreneur Donald Trump (once given a brief presidential buildup), who later married Marla Maples. This same program also included a segment on heroes of the Gulf War, which although human interest oriented had political overtones.

"20/20" PROGRAMMING DURING 1991

Selected programming during 1991 on "20/20" will be analyzed chronologically. Politically and diplomatically speaking, 1991 was the year of Desert Storm, continuing Middle East negotiations and the lull before the violence in the Balkans. Domestically, the economy was laggard.

Lynn Sherr conducted an interview and narration for a May 24, 1991, segment about Jane Hudson, described as "Abortion Doctor." The interview's focus and narration noted that despite legal rights to abortion, as a practical matter fewer medical people practiced abortion because of widespread anti-abortion agitation. The focus on Dr. Hudson was about elements of her practice, which had been in progress ever since President Franklin D. Roosevelt's administration. She had a Mayo fellowship and was a pioneer in pregnancy testing. The interview used the probing style of Barbara Walters, in which she asks surprising or startling questions to loosen up the subject of the interview. The doctor's worry about illegal abortions preceded her work, according to the interview. The background given was appropriate for such an interview, and like most media interviews for such programs, it paid a good deal of attention to controversial aspects of the topic. It could be considered under the criminal justice category because of the frequent involvement of the courts in the abortion issue.

The other segments of the program on that date dealt with other topics including the recently divorced Ivana Trump, formerly wed to New York's Plaza Hotel entrepreneur, and a human interest feature on war heroes (this was aired only three months after the end of the Persian Gulf War).

Barbara Walters and Hugh Downs on the September 20, 1991, "20/20" presented a segment by Lynn Sherr of ABC on pension swindles by private companies (a topic of legislative proposals in Congress); although it dealt with the private sector, it was related to reform proposals.

In the second part Hugh Downs discussed a *Money* magazine survey of American and foreign standards of living. This was economic in nature but definitely related to tax policy.

"20/20" PROGRAMMING DURING 1992

The first "20/20" program selected for analysis during 1992 dealt with the divorce proceeding involving another ABC correspondent, Joan Lunden of "Good Morning America." This was a personality-based interview, but the content of the program focused on the relatively novel idea of the woman breadwinner paying alimony to her husband, and what the appropriate arrangements would be for such a relationship. This fell under the civil justice heading, with domestic relations courts involved, but it also involved a well-known personality and an interesting sociological tendency in modern American society.

The March 27, 1992, "20/20" featured an interview with Leona Helmsley on her tax evasion case. This was the trial in which the hotel entrepreneur was accused of saying that "only the little people pay taxes," a statement she denied making. When Mrs. Helmsley went to prison, her husband dimmed the lights on New York's Empire State Building.

The second part of this program dealt with the events in the life of a released murderer.

The program for April 3, 1992, dealt with testimony on the John F. Kennedy assassination. The second portion dealt with "green card" immigrants in the United States who were threatened with deportation.

April 10, 1992, brought a program examining the privacy problems of Arthur Ashe, the tennis star who developed AIDS through exposure to tainted blood during surgery. This was followed by "The Victim Within," dealing with problems of CIA personnel and those who cooperate with them; "The Toughest Prison," on the problem of dealing with inmates in the Marion, Illinois, federal reformatory, and "Moles in the CIA That Weren't Moles," a different aspect of the intelligence agency dealing with its former administrator, James Jesus Angleton, who was dismissed by Director William Colby because of Angleton's paranoid attitude toward agents.

BARBARA WALTERS INTERVIEWS PEROT

On May 29, 1992, a considerable portion of "20/20" was devoted to H. Ross Perot, the computer magnate (founder of EDS and onetime General Motors board member) who conducted an Independent candidacy for the presidency. Barbara Walters conducted the Perot interview. The content which drew greatest attention from the press was probably a reference to Perot's intention never to employ a homosexual or anyone involved in marital infidelity. He would not appoint either, Perot told Barbara Walters. This drew much attention in media of all types. Perot did not mention that there is a difference between accusations about such matters and proof of them.[2]

The Walters interview examined Perot's small-town background, which was a subject of discussion in newspapers such as the *New York Times* and the *Washington Post*. The latter at one point made comparisons with the Clinton candidacy.

The analysis focused on Texarkana, Texas, and Perot's father's work as a cotton broker. It seemed aimed at satisfying the public's curiosity about a man who had been known primarily in a business context (head of a Texas computer firm which was taken over by General Motors) and about his activities since his widely covered departure from General Motors. Walters noted Perot's phenomenal rise in the polls and focused questions on his wife, Margot, and his career at the U.S. Naval Academy in Annapolis. The Perot interview was in a pattern one would expect for public figures making a race for national office. Much background and "buildup" material is usually included in such program segments. (A historical example in print is the quick buildup given internationalist insurance executive Wendell Willkie by friendly newspapers in 1940.)

A second segment on the "20/20" program for May 29, 1992, was a John Stossel interview about a woman who had a daughter in an all-girls school. Single-sex schools have been the object of court battles, and thus the issue can be considered political in context.

More than a year after the end of the Persian Gulf War, ABC's "20/20" featured on Friday, August 28, 1992, an interview with British citizens upset about a "friendly fire" error in the war zone which resulted in accidental death and injury to British combat troops. This incident was the focus of an investigation by authorities in both countries and a concern of allied diplomacy. This resembled similar actions in Vietnam (indeed, they appear to have occurred in every war). The allegation was that the casualties occurred during desert tank warfare.

This segment had a strong human interest element, and it played on the continuing public attention to the war and its aftermath. It occurred when the Bosnian civil war was just beginning to heat up, and interest in such matters continued to be strong.

A second part of the August 28 broadcast dealt with corporate cover-ups and whistle-blowers. A third feature, "Children in the Same Bed," did not appear to have political significance.

Friday, September 4, 1992, Hugh Downs presided over a program which included an extensive look at the dilemma of a Texas minister placed on trial for the alleged killing of his wife. Again the criminal justice theme which runs through all magazine programs we have examined was evident. The defendant was not convicted in this case. Both points of view were presented, in conformance with standards of fairness in journalism.

Friday, September 11, 1992, with Downs and Walters, brought a feature narrated by Tom Jarriell on boat people in Vietnam. This lengthy feature, much in need of editing, possessed a good deal of human interest and treated the story of a refugee woman who fled Saigon during the 1975 evacuation and eventually ended up in the United States. Her homecoming visit was described. More than half the program was devoted to this subject; if it had been tightly edited it could have been presented in twenty minutes, but it appeared that the producers thought this was a good story, "so let's give it everything." The same program included the segment "The Hidden Scandal," about environmental issues.

On September 25, 1992, Barbara Walters aired the second part of the Schwarzkopf interview. It is not an uncommon thing for networks to divide up lengthy interviews into more than one program, much as print interviews as in *The New Yorker* or prestige newspapers are broken up into serial form. This interview focused on the book in progress by the general (later titled *It Doesn't Take a Hero*) and on his prospective activities in the future.

Other features on September 25, 1992, included a segment on then–Arkansas Governor Bill Clinton and a human interest segment about Gregory Kay, a youth who was suing his parents for divorce.

On November 20, 1992, "20/20" featured a segment "The Skin Game" (essentially non-political); another on the daily life of police officers ("The Man Behind the Badge") and "Centenarians" (basically non-political).

On December 4, 1992, Barbara Walters interviewed the man convicted of John Lennon's murder, then incarcerated in Attica Prison in New York State. This was followed up by a moving segment on Florida victims of Hurricane Andrew. The first segment could be classified as criminal justice; the second one as government aid in emergency situations.

On Friday, December 11, 1992, Hugh Downs and Barbara Walters presented a program dealing with federal gun laws (clearly a criminal justice topic) and heart arrythmia. The latter was medical in nature, not political, but was doubtless brought forward by a news "peg" involving President George Bush, who had had a cardiac incident earlier (sometime in 1991) which caused some alarm for a brief period. The third segment concerned comedian Jerry Lewis, who was involved in a fundraising controversy.

DIANE SAWYER AND SAM DONALDSON ON "PRIMETIME LIVE"

The selection of programs for analysis on "PrimeTime Live" during 1991 and 1992 was limited to seven broadcasts. During these two years Sam Donaldson and Diane Sawyer co-anchored the show. The show supplemented "20/20" and it had its peak popularity in early 1994 when the magazine format apparently reached its high in public favor.

One of the highlights of "PrimeTime Live" during 1991 was Diane Sawyer's coverage of the abortive coup in Moscow, during which she gained a very brief interview with Russian Federation President Boris Yeltsin; this was followed up by a tour of the inside of the Kremlin, which she conducted a few months later, before the Soviet Union faded into oblivion. ABC News made this material available on videotape.

On February 7, 1991, Diane Sawyer interviewed General Norman Schwarzkopf. There was some speculation at the time that correspondents Sawyer and Walters were in competition to line up the general for an interview. However, neither the correspondents nor the network would comment on this situation.

The Diane Sawyer interview with General Schwarzkopf largely duplicated material that was in the Walters interview. At that time, the media's focus was squarely on Gulf War figures; a good comparison would be the media's scrutiny of the O. J. Simpson double murder trial in 1995. The public's strong interest explains the tendency to duplicate interviews with Gulf War figures. The military was censoring information at this time, so the Pentagon controlled interviewers' access to military leaders.[3]

On Thursday, September 19, 1991, Diane Sawyer interviewed a key player in Middle East diplomacy, President Hafez Assad of Syria. She was better prepared than in the interview with Yeltsin, which was essentially a catch-as-catch-can affair. Sam Donaldson joined in this program.

November 14, 1991, "PrimeTime Live" resembled "60 Minutes" when it presented a profile of a whistle-blower. A non-political segment featured basketball player Magic Johnson.

The August 13, 1992, "PrimeTime Live" contained four segments on the civil war in the former Yugoslavia (with Bosnian, Croatian and Serbian participants) and the death of an ABC producer killed there, a reminder that the media carry their share of combat casualties.

The September 3, 1992, "PrimeTime Live" featured a segment on the continuing controversy over fund-raising for muscular dystrophy by comedian Jerry Lewis.

October 8, 1992, "PrimeTime Live" topics included "Bryan's Murder in New York" about a Utah tennis fan killed in the New York subways, a feature on Madonna (non-political), and a segment on the "Presidential Debates," participated in by President Bush, Governor Clinton and H. Ross Perot.

"DATELINE NBC" PROGRAMMING IN 1992

Despite much publicity in print media and on other networks, "Dateline NBC" did broadcast programs other than that concerning the General Motors truck explosion which prompted an on-air apology.

On "Dateline NBC" program for Tuesday, September 8, 1992, Jane Pauley and Stone Phillips featured stories on a child abducted by a parent without custody and an interview by Pauley with Hillary Clinton, who was about to become first lady but at that time was a governor's wife.

The Pauley-Phillips team on "Dateline NBC" on September 15, 1992, built the program around information about the latest scandal involving Neil Bush, the President's son, and the Small Business Administration. Some minor disciplinary action was taken against Bush, but he was never in court as a result of this scandal.

The same program on Tuesday, November 11, 1992, discussed police brutality, a topic with both political and sociological implications, and the clearly non-political topic of "Passionate Sex in Marriage."

Topics dealt with by Phillips and Pauley on December 1, 1992, on "Dateline NBC" included homeopathy, bank robberies, and what was termed "a real world make believe" (virtual reality).

Stone Phillips and Jane Pauley on "Dateline NBC" for Tuesday, December 15, 1992, discussed rapists and parole, and kidnap victims.

The basic categories of these segments include criminal justice, crime, interviews with celebrities including political celebrities, and exposé stories such as those about police brutality and scandals. The personality orientation of these stories makes it clear that each of these three programs, "20/20," "PrimeTime Live" and "Dateline NBC," has the principal characteristics of electronic magazines.

In the next chapter, ratings and audience information about these shows will be examined in an effort to clarify the nature of these programs and the kind of audience each one attracts.

NOTES

1. Telephone interview with Mr. Alan Wurtzel, senior vice president for news magazines and long-form programming, ABC News, conducted on Wednesday, April 13, 1994.

2. "20/20," May 29, 1992, quotations from Journal Graphics transcript. Barbara Walters also conducted a Perot interview on Friday, October 2, 1992, in which Perot told her he was "aiming for 50" in his campaign. He also said his campaign would be "unconventional." "Ross Perot Speaks with Barbara Walters," excerpt from "20/20" October 2, 1992, program on Prodigy Interactive Service, October 4, 1992, also available from Journal Graphics. Other "20/20" programs are listed in Appendix IV. Also see Steve McClellan, "ABC News Is Number One, But . . . : Survey Shows Network to Be the Best, but News Execs Say It's Not Perfect," *Broadcasting & Cable* 123, no. 19 (September 27, 1993): pp. 41, 42.

3. For background see Stanley A. Renshon, *The Political Psychology of the Gulf War: Leaders, Publics, and the Process of Conflict* (Pittsburgh: University of Pittsburgh Press, 1993). Also see the following: Marcia Lynn Whicker, James P. Pfiffner, and Raymond A. Moore, eds., *The Presidency and the Persian Gulf War* (Westport, CT: Praeger, 1993), and Robert Denton, Jr., *Television Coverage of the Persian Gulf War* (Westport, CT: Praeger, 1993).

Chapter Nine

Audience Rankings (1985–1993)— Interpreting Data

Data for each program compiled from weekly rankings, audience share and homes using television give some useful insights into the growth of magazine programming. The weekly rankings data are presented in Tables 1 through 10 in the Appendix at the end of this chapter.

During 1985 programs that were tracked were "60 Minutes," "20/20" and "ABC News Closeup." The latter was not a true magazine show, but it was used to compare the rankings with those of traditional documentary programming.

There was one preemption for "20/20" (a problem in interpreting the Nielsen data, for example, among others, is the fact that the networks sometimes test out new programs with a gingerly caution, making gaps in quarterly measurements). However, "60 Minutes" led in rankings all through the four quarters of 1985 with the exception of a few times late in the second quarter. Events which occurred during this year included the taking of hostages in Lebanon, a TWA hostage-taking episode, the continuing Iran-Iraq War and the early beginnings of glasnost in the post-Brezhnev Soviet Union.

Other programs measured during this year included "West 57th" on CBS, then fairly new; a "Barbara Walters Special" and an ABC News special on the hostages. An early version of "48 Hours" (a new approach to programming referred to then by some as "reality programming") was examined.

As counterpoint for this measurement of network programming, some scattered monthly audience share data from CNN, the spot news cable network, were used.

During 1986, four programs measured were "60 Minutes," "20/20," "West 57th" and the NBC production "1986."

Some patterns emerge from looking at network data. The most consistent network insofar as regular carrying of the programming was ABC, a pattern which may reflect the journalistic background of the owners of Capital Cities Broadcasting, long in the radio business before the 1986 takeover of ABC. The CBS programming reflects the effort put into building programs like "60 Minutes" and "48 Hours," but there are more preemptions caused by special events like the Olympics, the Country Music Awards and public affairs events such as the nominating conventions (the latter caused preemptions on all three traditional networks). It ought to be noted that Fox network does not appear in these early ratings.

During this time in the universe of news programming, ratings leadership on the evening news broadcasts passed from CBS to ABC. However, new developments such as the gradual growth in influence of "Nightline" and the moving of news programming all across the weekly schedule of dayparts (hourly segments of the broadcast day) put this news leadership into a somewhat different perspective. As one network developed news leadership (at least in evening news dominance) the other sought to develop sports programming dominance. The carrying of "soft news" programming on NBC (until 1992 and 1993, when "Now with Tom and Katie" and "Dateline NBC" began to appear with consistency) was much more sporadic, indicating perhaps that other priorities were those most in evidence at the "senior network." Our research did not look into the impact of the new ownership of NBC by General Electric.

One question future researchers might wish to consider is whether this factor was important to an apology given by NBC when a program on a faulty truck manufactured by General Motors stirred a controversy and a threat of a lawsuit. Occasionally, network litigation involves factors like those of a CBS lawsuit that was filed to seek an injunction to bar a South Dakota judge in 1994 from banning a piece of tape (hidden camera) taken inside a controversial packing plant. ABC went to court or at least engaged in a legal dispute with Food Lion supermarkets over a similar controversy. The previous controversies engaged in by CBS included a legal battle not involving magazine programs but "CBS Reports" and the long controversy between CBS and General William Westmoreland regarding the "Vietnam Deception" program. This occurred about the same time that *Time* magazine was being sued by General Ariel Sharon of Israel for David Levy's reporting with statements based on interpretation of classified Israeli material about the Sabra and Shattilla massacre in Lebanon in 1982. (Levy was then *Time*'s correspondent in the area.)

In 1986 "60 Minutes" continued its dominance, but the figures indicate a growing audience for "20/20" and some new interest in "West 57th," which more than one critic said was aimed at the "yuppie" audience. Events in 1986 which got some coverage on networks included the Iran-Contra scandal and some shakeups in the second Reagan administration.

By 1987, the same programs were still seeking audience share. Ted Koppel of "Nightline" was a figure of growing importance in network news coverage, and in some of the accompanying tables, his specials have been contrasted with the magazine programs we have measured. Among other events occurring in 1987 was the Wall Street crash in October of that year.

The leader in 1988 was "60 Minutes."

In 1989, the major programs were "60 Minutes," "20/20," "West 57th," and "48 Hours." But ABC was soon to introduce "PrimeTime Live," which appeared in the third quarter of the year. The year saw the beginning of the Bush Administration; the start of the Resolution Trust Corporation (RTC), which sought to end the savings and loan bailout; and in Europe the collapse of the Berlin Wall and the end of Romanian strongman Nikolai Caecescu's rule, among other events. The Asian area saw the Tin An Men Square uprising in Peking (Beijing) and new tensions between the United States and China.

By 1990 "PrimeTime Live" was beginning to build an audience. It featured as anchors Diane Sawyer (formerly with CBS and earlier on President Nixon's staff) and Sam Donaldson. One of its most widely viewed programs focused on the art treasures inside the Kremlin. The same year NBC was trying one of its many magazine experiments with "Exposé." The program brought on support and criticism based on material developed about Virginia Senator Charles S. Robb. The early work of Connie Chung (who came to CBS from NBC) was featured on "Saturday Night with Connie

Chung" and later on "Eye to Eye with Connie Chung." The magazine programming phenomenon was beginning to take on momentum.

When Jane Pauley shifted over from the morning "Today" show to evening programming she for a time anchored a program entitled "Real Life with Jane Pauley." Later she teamed with Stone Phillips to appear on "Dateline NBC," but this had not yet occurred in 1989. Maria Shriver (formerly with CBS) worked for NBC in a new magazine program, "First Person with Maria Shriver." Similarities can be noted between these programs and the Chung and Barbara Walters showcases, but except for an occasional political or military celebrity, they did not usually feature political figures. The year brought the Iraqi invasion of Kuwait and the crisis which eventually led to the Gulf war of early 1991.

The 1991 programming led to further growth of featured programming; the spread of magazine programs to every night of the schedule was almost complete. In that year the original two offerings had grown to a list including "PrimeTime Live," "Real Life with Jane Pauley," "Exposé," "48 Hours," "First Person with Maria Shriver," and "Face to Face with Connie Chung." The Gulf War monopolized the media attention during early 1991, and this preoccupation was reflected to some extent in the content of programs already discussed.

In the political year of 1992, much attention was paid to the three-way campaign (closest to 1912 in the showing of the third candidate, in contrast to 1980 and 1968, as well as 1924). It was not until 1993 that Forrest Sawyer (formerly with CBS) began to develop "Day One" as a new magazine program. He was later joined by former CBS correspondent Meredith Vieira.

We have traced through some of the available data the growth of programming since the introduction of "60 Minutes" in 1968. Before concluding the chapter we will discuss briefly the 25th anniversary of this landmark program by examining and analyzing the content of its November anniversary program.

A SUMMARY OF "60 MINUTES" PROGRAMMING OVER 25 YEARS

During the 1993 November "sweeps" "60 Minutes" ranked second on the week of November 1–7 with 21.1 audience share and 33 million homes using television (HUT). In the data for November 15–21 the same program ranked first and generated 22.4 audience share with 35 million HUT. The final part of the sweeps month was reflected in data for the November 29–December 5 period which placed the program third with 21.2 audience share and 33 million HUT. Thus "60 Minutes" was in the top three each week.[1]

It was during this month that "60 Minutes" aired its 25th anniversary program. While it featured correspondents (and that was not surprising), it provided a kind of catalog of political figures between 1968, the year Richard Nixon defeated Hubert Humphrey and George Wallace for the presidency, and 1993, the first year of the Clinton administration.

Steve Kroft narrated an outtake from the spring 1992 program in which the Clintons were interviewed and showed a startling occurrence. As Kroft described it, "It was like an artillery round going off. And then I suddenly realized that the lights had fallen off the wall and almost killed them."[2]

Another episode described is that in which H. Ross Perot, the independent candidate for the presidency, almost walked off the set when piqued by a question from Lesley Stahl.[3]

Mike Wallace, lead interviewer, was shown in kinescope from the early television era (1950s) interviewing Eleanor Roosevelt.[4] Another Wallace interview, with Jimmy Carter, was included in a brief clip.[5]

Charles Kuralt's interview of retired Secret Service Agent Clint Hill (present in Dallas on November 22, 1963) was included.[6] A recapitulation was done of Lesley Stahl's interview with Dr. Susan Wickland and her harassment by the organization Lambs of Christ in the abortion controversy.[7]

Footage from Morley Safer's Vietnam coverage was a part of this program (he began with "60 Minutes" in 1970).[8]

A Dan Rather interview with Fidel Castro, the Cuban strongman, dealt with reports about a Soviet combat brigade in Cuba.[9] Charles Kuralt also referred to ridicule aimed at Rather for using a native costume during the Afghan war.[10]

Producer Don Hewitt was referred to as the producer of the first of the 1960 televised Kennedy-Nixon debates.[11] Morley Safer's interview with a wrongly convicted woman in a Texas prison, Joyce Ann Brown, was a part of the montage.[12]

In segments dealing with diplomacy and military matters, one

interview with impact was that done by Harry Reasoner with a
Russian veteran of the Afghan war named Borovik.[13]

An environmental impact segment which dealt with an issue not
only of internal interest but also with a diplomatic impact was that
in which Charles Kuralt interviewed persons involved in the nuclear
disaster at Chernobyl.[14]

Footage was included of a Lesley Stahl interview with President
George Bush, as well as Ross Perot.[15]

Alcee Hastings, federal judge accused of taking a bribe, was
interviewed by Diane Sawyer during her CBS stint[16] (Hastings later
became a congressman). A Lesley Stahl interview with Russian
President Boris Yeltsin was referred to by Andy Rooney in a
segment included in the retrospective montage.[17]

The "60 Minutes" quarter-century retrospective was to a considerable degree a kind of promotion for the producing network, but
it also demonstrated quite well the way in which politics and
communication are intertwined, and it illustrated the by now well
known bromide that television has a different kind of impact than
print and radio. Part of the difficulty in analyzing a program of this
type is to determine where politics ends and where non-political
coverage begins.

The "60 Minutes" montage also did not deal (for obvious reasons)
with the internal politics of the world of broadcasting, something
which in today's environment carries in its own way as much
impact as the politics carried out in the public arena and in the
cloakrooms of Washington and the state capitals (not to mention
cities and counties around the nation).

To some extent, although not in detail, this program capsulized
the relatively brief history of the intertwining of broadcasting and
politics. In the future world of interactive cable, there will doubtless
be nostalgia for the early television era, much as people in the first
years of television had (at least in the industry) some degree of
nostalgia for the "Front Page" heyday of print.

One point to remember in analyzing mass communication of the
type represented by the traditional networks is that elite publications (journals, prestige newspapers, serious magazines) still carry
a good deal of weight with leadership elites in various segments of
society (this is nothing new).

However, electronic magazine programs need to be analyzed in
the context of total communication. Industry structure and govern-

mental and political institutions are all elements in the dynamic interaction between public officials (both elected and appointed) and the institutions and people who filter their actions to the general public and to specialized audiences.

The measurements made by audience rating organizations are imperfect at best. But the whole idea of accountability in a democratic system calls for assessments of media actors as well as elected officials and staffs. The interaction that occurs between them will be a continuing process, so long as the present system lasts.

One final comment might be made before conclusions are drawn in Chapter Ten: The current importance of broadcast and interactive media, as the turn of the twenty-first century approaches, reflects a broader global trend, and that is the encroachment of private entities (such as multi-national broadcasting, telephone and cable operations—CBS, NBC, ABC, CNN, BBC, and others) on what was once national political sovereignty. The media networking around the globe coincides with an erosion of national sovereignty as well in ceding some authority to international entities such as the United Nations, NATO, and other international combines. Thus the landscape of communications differs greatly from its beginning as the twentieth century draws to an end.

APPENDIX

Table 1
Magazine Program Rankings, 1985

	1st qtr.	2nd qtr.	3rd qtr.	4th qtr.
60 Minutes	8.5	13.3	10.7	6.7
20/20	43.4	27.1	13.9	41.8
ABC Closeup	62.0	—	—	—
B W Special	—	3.0	—	—
ABC Hostages	—	—	59.0	—
48 Hours	—	—	—	10.0
Crossfire (CNN)	Jan. 1.4, Feb. 1.3, Mar. 1.4, Apr. 1.4, May 1.3, Jun. 1.4, Jul. 1.4, Aug. 1.1, Sept. 1.0, Oct. 1.2, Nov. 1.5, Dec. 1.4			

Sources: Network Data, *Broadcasting* for 1985; CNN Data, Turner Broadcasting

Table 2
Magazine Program Rankings, 1986

	1st qtr.	2nd qtr.	3rd qtr.	4th qtr.
60 Minutes	6.1	14.2	8.2	—
20/20	31.9	18.4	24.1	—
West 57th	—	43.2	59.0	—
1986 (NBC)	—	37.4	52.2	—

Source: *Broadcasting* for 1986

Table 3
Magazine Program Rankings, 1987

	1st qtr.	2nd qtr.	3rd qtr.	4th qtr.
60 Minutes	6.5	11.6	17.3	8.3
20/20	42.2	30.5	16.3	43.3
CBS Reports	—	—	—	68.0
Jennings/Koppel Report	—	—	—	67.0
B W Special	—	—	26.0	6.0
West 57th	—	59.7	58.8	67.5

Source: *Broadcasting* for 1987

Table 4
Magazine Program Rankings, 1988

	1st qtr.	2nd qtr.	3rd qtr.	4th qtr.
60 Minutes	11.6	11.4	10.0	5.8
20/20	42.6	34.1	21.3	32.8
48 Hours	48.9	56.2	41.2	53.3
West 57th	62.2	62.0	52.0	—
NBC News Special	41.0	—	—	—
ABC News Closeup	—	—	33.0	—
B W Special	—	5.0	7.0	—
Probe ABC	—	65.0	—	—
CBS Reports: Wall Within	—	53.0	—	—
CBS Pres. Debate Analyses	—	—	21.0	39.0
ABC Pres. Debate Analyses	—	—	39.0	43.0

Source: *Broadcasting* for 1988

Table 5
Magazine Program Rankings, 1989

	1st qtr.	2nd qtr.	3rd qtr.	4th qtr.
60 Minutes	9.8	11.8	15.4	7.8
20/20	34.3	28.3	25.4	33.1
48 Hours	48.3	53.0	47.1	51.5
West 57th	65.9	63.8	44.0	—
Koppel Report	56.0	—	—	—
PrimeTime Live	—	—	41.6	—
Sat. Night with Connie Chung	—	—	—	—
Crossfire (CNN)	Jan. 1.2, Feb. 1.1, Mar. 1.1, Apr. 0.9, May 0.9, Jun. 0.9			

Sources: Magazine Program Data, *Broadcasting* for 1989;
CNN Data, Turner Broadcasting

Table 6
Magazine Program Rankings, 1990

	1st qtr.	2nd qtr.	3rd qtr.	4th qtr.
60 Minutes	7.6	11.2	5.8	5.5
20/20	36.8	29.1	20.8	40.3
PrimeTime Live	64.9	52.7	42.1	60.1
48 Hours	70.9	49.8	50.0	69.4
48 Hours Special	—	—	28.0	—
Sat. Night with Connie Chung	70.5	70.8	—	—
Face to Face with Connie Chung	—	—	33.6	—
Exposé (NBC)	—	31.0	—	—
Real Life/Jane Pauley	—	—	19.8	64.0
Jennings/Iraq	—	—	39.0	—
Koppel Report	—	—	67.0	—
1st Person/Maria Shriver	—	—	—	68.0
Crossfire (CNN)	Jan. 1.6, Feb. 1.2, Mar. 1.2, Jul. 0.9, Aug. 1.7, Sept. 1.4, Oct. 1.5, Nov. 1.5, Dec. 1.4			

Sources: Magazine Program Data, *Broadcasting* for 1990;
CNN Data, Turner Broadcasting

Table 7
Magazine Program Rankings, 1991

	1st qtr.	2nd qtr.	3rd qtr.	4th qtr.
60 Minutes	5.4	5.7	3.6	2.5
20/20	27.5	20.7	21.6	24.5
PrimeTime Live	52.3	43.5	38.6	48.9
Real Life/Jane Pauley	67.7	69.0	73.7	80.0
Exposé (NBC)	64.3	69.8	79.2	89.0
48 Hours	57.3	32.5	31.4	44.3
20/20 Special	—	27.0	—	—
1st Person/Maria Shriver	34.5	33.0	—	34.0
Face to Face with Connie Chung	48.0	—	—	—
B W Special	—	—	20.0	—
Crossfire (CNN)	Apr. 1.3, May 1.0, Jun. 0.8, Jul. 0.9, Aug. 1.2, Sept. 1.0, Oct. 1.3, Nov. 1.1, Dec. 1.2			

Sources: Magazine Program Data, *Broadcasting* for 1991;
          CNN Data, Turner Broadcasting

Table 8
Magazine Program Rankings, 1992

	1st qtr.	2nd qtr.	3rd qtr.	4th qtr.
60 Minutes	1.8	7.0	5.3	2.2
20/20	25.2	41.0	16.9	14.1
PrimeTime Live	34.6	11.0	18.1	21.1
Day One	—	—	—	—
48 Hours	27.0	23.0	6.0	29.6
NBC Special/Cuban Crisis	78.0	—	—	—
Dateline NBC	—	—	47.7	46.0
West 57th	—	—	—	—
Story Behind the Story (NBC)	60.0	—	—	—
1st Person/Maria Shriver	45.0	—	—	—
Another World (NBC)	78.0	—	—	—
Brokaw Report	74.0	—	80.0	—
Missile Crisis (ABC)	—	—	—	64.0

Source: *Broadcasting* for 1992

Table 9
Magazine Program Rankings, 1993

	1st qtr.	2nd qtr.	3rd qtr.	4th qtr.
60 Minutes	20.0	6.8	4.2	2.9
20/20	23.3	16.2	8.2	19.6
PrimeTime Live	15.3	16.6	7.5	16.8
48 Hours	31.0	20.1	10.8	38.2
Day One	40.0	52.4	30.0	35.7
Dateline NBC	52.2	26.6	14.9	44.9
Eye to Eye with Connie Chung	—	20.0	18.4	56.4
ABC Special	51.0	—	—	—
NBC Special	40.0	—	—	—

Source: Broadcasting and Cable, 1993

Table 10
1994–1995 First Season Advance Magazine Schedule

	ABC	CBS	NBC
Monday 10–11 P.M.	Day One		
Tuesday 10–11 P.M.			Dateline NBC
Wednesday 10–11 P.M.	Turning Point		
Thursday 9–10 P.M.		Eye to Eye with Connie Chung	
Thursday 10–11 P.M.	PrimeTime Live		
Friday 9–10 P.M.			Dateline NBC II
Friday 10–11 P.M.	20/20		
Sunday 7–8 P.M.		60 Minutes	

Note: Fox had "Front Page" in 1993–1994.

Source: TV Guide, 42, no. 23 (June 4, 1994): p. 38.

NOTES

1. Data from *Broadcasting & Cable* issues of November and December 1993.
2. Transcript: CBS News, "60 Minutes" XXVI, no. 9 (November 14, 1993): p. 2.
3. *Ibid.*

4. *Ibid.*, p. 3.
5. *Ibid.*, p. 5.
6. *Ibid.*, pp. 8–10.
7. *Ibid.*, pp. 11–13.
8. *Ibid.*, p. 16.
9. *Ibid.*, pp. 19, 20.
10. *Ibid.*, p. 20.
11. *Ibid.*, p. 25.
12. *Ibid.*, pp. 31, 32.
13. *Ibid.*, p. 34.
14. *Ibid.*, p. 36.
15. *Ibid.*, pp. 37, 38.
16. *Ibid.*, p. 40.
17. *Ibid.*, p. 48.

Chapter Ten

"Tabloids" versus Magazine Programs: Networks' Role as Standard Setters

Later in this chapter, an assessment will be made of television network magazine programming as it exists in the mid-1990s. However, a brief discussion will follow about the distinction between electronic magazines and their "tabloid" competitors. Some of the discussion reflects a dialog between the author and Andrew Heyward of CBS News, previously executive producer of "Eye to Eye with Connie Chung" and now executive producer of "The CBS Evening News." Some of the conclusions reflect the author's overview of the content analysis and ratings examination covered in preceding chapters.

Mr. Heyward, who also formerly produced "48 Hours," found a clear distinction between network magazines and the kinds of tabloids produced by syndicates. He commented:

There are superficial similarities between "tabloid" syndicated shows and network magazine productions, as similar subjects are dealt with on both. However, there is a fundamental difference in the first principles of these shows. The networks must, like the syndicated shows, satisfy the public appetite, and they are also subject to profit maximization. But unlike the syndicated tabloid shows which must stand or fall only on the ratings, the networks combine the profit-making necessity with a standard-setting goal; they must set a standard for public service while making a profit and staying competitive.

We must determine whether a story belongs on "Eye to Eye." Some of the competing newsmagazines went overboard on the stories about the

Menendez brothers [California murder suspects in parents' slayings] and John and Lorena Bobbitt [in a Virginia sexual mutilation case], which were criminal justice stories. Our approach had a different standard. Bernard Goldberg, our correspondent, tried to put these stories into the framework of "finding an excuse" for criminal activity, a "Don't Blame Me" attitude.

Goldberg's work was so original that CBS is carrying a one-hour special later this month [May 1994]; the original story developed into seeing a pattern of escape from responsibility. There is intrinsic news value in this theme of the subversion of justice by making excuses. The defendants shun accountability in criminal trials. This kind of examination of underlying social trends is part of CBS' responsibility to uphold its traditions by setting standards for the industry.

This is different from what some of the competing networks did, which is showing night after night coverage of the Menendez or Bobbitt cases without getting to the real story, which is how defense attorneys can manipulate trial juries in such a way as to subvert the judicial process. These are two good examples of how a network can serve the public interest while providing news coverage, when there is a bigger issue involved. The networks have the role of upholding journalistic merit and when we fail we ought to do better. If a story is of no merit, then we shouldn't carry it.

The "soft news" magazine boom is the result of the huge success of "PrimeTime Live" and "48 Hours" in the late '80s. This led to the development of more successful programming and besides ratings and profits it helped to generate respect and esteem for network programming in an age when cable has become an important factor with, to some degree, narrowcasting.[1] [Also, magazine shows compete with entertainment and in the prime time universe such programming is cheaper to produce than entertainment.]

In regard to specific programming topics, Mr. Heyward had the following comment:

It is a bit of a stretch to consider the Tonya Harding story a political story, even though she was called before a grand jury and the criminal justice system was involved. But the story does tap into an underlying social issue, the exploitation of sports and the extent to which some people will go to become a champion or a winner. This was a morality tale with glamorous, interesting and colorful characters. It is a story that tells us something about America in 1994.

Connie Chung got the story through tough, dogged reporting and hard work. She managed to make inroads into the Harding camp. You may recall that the exclusive interview was preceded by interviews with her father and mother and her coach. This was just good shoe-leather reporting—a story that the *Washington Post* or the *New York Times* would love to have had.

In the author's discussion with Mr. Heyward, the CBS producer was asked his opinion about the best segment done on "Eye to Eye with Connie Chung." Mr. Heyward commented:

The best segment we have probably done about a political figure was the coverage of President Clinton on the eve of the NAFTA [North American Free Trade Agreement] vote in Congress last year [1993]. It was an important story, but because Connie Chung got behind the scenes and explained the lobbying effort, it took an arcane issue and focused on how it was important to the American public. You must also remember in talking about "soft news" political coverage that any magazine is only a part of the network's product line, which has diversity, and it has to be considered in the context of political coverage on "Sunday Morning," "Face the Nation," and overall coverage. "CBS This Morning" touches on quite a few stories dealing with issues and policy. So a magazine has to be considered as a part of the whole range of programming which we offer as a network.

One problem in "soft news" is that we have to develop a product for prime time that the public will watch in preference to a "sitcom" or entertainment. So we must feature the human interest element; the evening is a time when many in the audience don't want to think about intrinsically serious topics, so we need a kind of "hook" to draw their attention which the human interest factor provides.

Mr. Heyward was asked to comment about magazine coverage of a range of political and diplomatic issues. His comments were as follows:

On Bosnia, Bob Simon did an excellent piece on the Siege of Sarajevo and how the lives of individuals were affected. We had another story about a Bosnian girl starting over in America; because this had more of a domestic theme it was a good audience attraction in the viewing environment I explained. Bosnia of course is a huge story with all kinds of human interest ramifications.

The only story done on the former Soviet Union was about an invasion by the Russian mob here in the United States, as part of the falling apart of the Soviet police state.

Our correspondents also got inside the training camps of the militant white separatists in South Africa.

On domestic issues, we have done stories on health care reform. We do a fair number of stories on this issue, as health care is a kind of staple on magazine shows. For example, we did the story of a woman who was in a bitter dispute with an HMO regarding the billing for her daughter's treatment. The HMO in turn accused her of child abuse, and this had a human interest angle. We did a story on assisted suicide. We also did a consumer-oriented story on how to control the vitamin and food supplement industries and protect the public interest in that area.

We have not dealt directly with reregulation of cable television, but we have presented stories that are of interest to the public [in the field of communications], for instance dealing with "infomercials" and home shopping on television.

I would suggest a new category for your analysis, which includes the stories we have done on "Eye to Eye" of which I am the proudest. [These] weren't on your original question list at all. These are the stories dealing with the quality of life in modern America, as developed by Bernard Goldberg. One such story was the segment done on the 30th anniversary of the Kennedy assassination in November, 1993, which compared the America of 1963 with that of 1993. This story grew out of Senator Daniel Patrick Moynihan's (D-New York) theme of the decline of civility in America. [Senator Moynihan has been a proponent of working to replace the present welfare system in America.]

Another such story with sociological underpinnings was the debate over the ideas of Charles Murray, the conservative social critic and author of *Losing Ground* and other books.

These are vital but not typical magazine stories and they often tackle the conventional wisdom.

Another theme of Goldberg's has been the backlash against "political correctness." We have covered activities of the Nation of Islam on college campuses and as previously mentioned the theme of subversion of accountability by use of excuses. We also looked at the Antioch College (Ohio) sexual correctness policy and how that represented a sociological phenomenon.[2]

Some conclusions can be drawn about two matters analyzed in this book: the evolution of electronic magazine programming on national networks in the United States and categories into which programs may be placed in terms of content.

In the nearly thirty years since the magazine format was first used on national network television with the advent of "60 Minutes," a dramatic progression has occurred. Long-form traditional documentaries were aired in pioneer days of television; the format gradually moved to a personality based, ratings driven type of programming known as the "magazine show." Additionally, the proportion of prime time devoted to this kind of presentation has grown. In early 1994 the magazine programming trend reached an apparent peak; there was at least one such program on the schedule each night of the week. In February 1994 ABC had signed a multi-year contract with Diane Sawyer reported to involve development of a same-network series of magazine programs on several week-nights in prime time. Saturation appeared near, causing some to wonder whether the category of magazine shows might meet the fate of earlier entertainment programs like westerns and police and medical stories.

The prime time development of electronic magazines has paralleled the growth of cable television, first as an adjunct to, and then finally as a communications medium approaching a position over-shadowing that of traditional broadcast television. Along with this has come the development of "electronic tabloids," sensation-oriented programming, mostly syndicated, which has pulled conventional broadcast programming in the direction of high-ratings, personality oriented content. This study does not deal with tabloids, except to mention that they have had a significant influence in fashioning network programming. The economics of the industry, which first brought restructuring in the 1980s and in the 1990s brought re-regulation of cable, has been the context in which these developments have occurred.

The specific programs analyzed herein have included, beyond pathbreaking "60 Minutes," such other CBS programs as "48 Hours," "Street Stories," "West 57th," "Eye to Eye with Connie Chung" and "Saturday Night with Connie Chung," as well as the short-lived "Verdict" with Rita Braver as anchor.[3]

ABC programming discussed at least briefly has included the pioneering "20/20," often psychologically oriented (ESP, soft feature material, personality based non-political, as well as exposés), "Prime-Time Live," and most recently, "Day One." This development has complemented the rise of ABC as a news leader, although CBS has not fully relinquished that role if all dayparts are considered. At the same time that ABC has taken over leadership of traditional evening news with "ABC World News Tonight" featuring Peter Jennings, and has developed the hard news program "Nightline," itself an outgrowth of the 1979–1981 hostage crisis in Iran, CBS has worked in the area of reality programming with the "48 Hours" format and its other magazines. Thus some important developments have been occurring; these have paralleled the electronic advances which have made possible new graphics and new production techniques which have made the basic documentary more interesting. As this has occurred, more of the traditional documentary work has been left to the Public Broadcasting Service (PBS).

As for program content, such basic categories as public policy, criminal justice and leadership personalities can be established. There is obviously some overlapping with these. But these are clearly the politically oriented themes used to air these broadcasts. Categorization is sometimes a bit muddy, as the coverage of the Nancy Kerrigan–Tonya Harding episode overstepped the boundaries of traditional sports coverage to enter the criminal justice category.

The inner conflict in all American television is more and more reflected in global programming, although CNN and other world-wide efforts at programming are not analyzed in depth in this study. This conflict is that between the public service ideal and the necessity for private sector production organizations to make a profit and to stay in business, as well as the urge to become a leader by being highly competitive.

This does not require any great polemicizing but is simply a reality of broadcast/cable programming in an era in which non-public communication is the dominant economic mode, and this is reflected in programming.

Public Broadcasting Service programming came into being in the United States to supplement more traditional commercial network programming to create a dual system, just as ITN and other private enterprise networks (complementing the subscription BBC in the United Kingdom) have developed around the world.

As the former Soviet Union moved into a partly privatized economy this same kind of dual programming was present, unless one argues that the collapse of communism resulted in supplanting "Vremya"-type presentations with enterprise-oriented news coverage.

It must be concluded, then, that politically oriented program-ming is market driven, that it has been impacted by electronic technology changes, but also that it must be analyzed in the eco-nomic context of programming.

As programming moves from the present day cable and conven-tional broadcast content to a satellite/fiberoptic kind of communication or some unforeseen new technology, one may expect either a continuation of the trends discussed here or, given new environmental factors, a reversal of these trends. Only the future can determine this, but it is the duty of persons making serious academic studies to make an effort at prediction, no matter how hazy conclusions may be or how difficult.

These findings represent the outcome of our study of magazine program content in looking at soft news evolution on national network television in the United States.[4]

NOTES

1. Comments quoted from telephone interview by author with Mr. Andrew Heyward, then executive producer of CBS' "Eye to Eye with Connie Chung," Friday, May 13, 1994.

2. Further quotations from Friday, May 13, 1994, telephone interview with Andrew Heyward of CBS.

3. It may be noted that in connection with the short-lived "Verdict" featuring the coverage of Rita Braver and other CBS correspondents, a cable network, Court TV, recently begun, has had considerable success with this type of programming and has issued a series of videotapes with court programs.

4. CBS continues to experiment with magazine programming in prime time. "America Tonight" aired in summer 1994 and a new two-hour format has been tried on a pilot basis. ABC has introduced "Turning Point" and NBC has added "Dateline NBC II." The mushrooming trend had apparently peaked early in 1994.

Appendix I

"60 Minutes" Broadcasts

All Burrelle's and Journal Graphics transcripts contain references to audio only, including voiceover and microphone instructions. Where special transcripts with camera work were recorded, the work was done by a special assistant to the author, Anita Kay Darnes.

"60 MINUTES" 1991 PROGRAMS

January 20, 1991: Saddam's Bodyguard: The Man Who Armed Iraq; Inferno; Iraqi Terror; A Few Minutes with Andy Rooney (XXIII: 19) (New York: Journal Graphics, 1991) Program # 2319

January 27, 1991: Stormin' Norman; Chemical Warfare; The Secret of the Gara Mountains; The Best Stuff; Iran, Iraq and the U.S. (XIII: 20) (New York: Journal Graphics, 1991) Program # 2320

February 3, 1991: The German Connection; Moscow; The Palestinians; A Few Minutes with Andy Rooney (XXIII: 21) (New York: Journal Graphics, 1991) Program # 2321

February 10, 1991: The Saudis; Jane's; Tuning In; Red Cross Blood; A Few Minutes with Andy Rooney (XXIII: 22) Program # 2322

February 17, 1991: A Letter from Jermarr; Piece of the Pie; Waddington TV; A Few Minutes with Andy Rooney (XXIII: 23) Program # 2323

February 24, 1991: Waiting to Go Home; Becky's Story; Gulf War Update; A Few Minutes with Andy Rooney (XXIII: 24) Program # 2324

March 3, 1991: Free at Last!; Werner Erhard; My Family Is Missing; A Few Minutes with Andy Rooney (XXIII: 25) Program # 2325 (Anita Darnes Audio/Video Transcript)

March 10, 1991: Another Saddam?; The Moscow Mystique; The Birmingham Six; A Few Minutes with Andy Rooney (XXIII: 26) Program # 2326

March 24, 1991: Saddam's Billions; The Numbers Game; The Trials of Michael Dowd; A Few Minutes with Andy Rooney (XXIII: 28) Program # 2328

March 31, 1991: Raw Land, Raw Deal; The New Plantations; School for Judges; A Few Minutes with Andy Rooney (XXIII: 29) Program # 2329

April 7, 1991: Brucification; Stray Voltage; Watch Out for Herman Wrice; A Few Minutes with Andy Rooney (XXIII: 30) Program # 2330

April 21, 1991: You Own It!; War Games; Susanne Logan's Story; A Few Minutes with Andy Rooney (XXIII: 32) Program # 2332

May 5, 1991: Oxford House; Prison U.; U.S. Marshal; A Few Minutes with Andy Rooney (XXIII: 34) Program # 2334

May 12, 1991: Clark M. Clifford; Playing War; Doctor Forman; A Few Minutes with Andy Rooney (XXIII: 35) Program # 2335

May 26, 1991: Danger; Vietnam 101; The Brady Bunch; A Few Minutes with Andy Rooney (XXIII: 37) Program # 2337

June 2, 1991: RU-486; Underworld; Blonde Ambition; A Few Minutes with Andy Rooney (XXIII: 38) Program # 2338

June 9, 1991: "This House Is a Steal"; Dr. Brooks; The Pollards; A Few Minutes with Andy Rooney (XXIII: 39) Program # 2339

June 16, 1991: Mustard Gas; Mayor Moran; Manhunt; A Few Minutes with Andy Rooney (XXIII: 40) Program # 2340

June 23, 1991: Voyage of Discovery; Joseph Stalin and Slava; Moscow, CCCP-TV in Moscow and Telling the Truth (XXIII: 41) Program # 2341

June 30, 1991: Bad Cops; "I Know It When I See It"; Needle Park; A Few Minutes with Andy Rooney (XXIII: 42) Program # 2342

July 14, 1991: Becky's Story; Paul Simon; The Trials of Michael Dowd; A Few Minutes with Andy Rooney (XXIII: 44) Program # 2344

July 28, 1991: Ward 5A; Oliver's Story; My Family Is Missing; A Few Minutes with Andy Rooney (XXIII: 46) Program # 2346

August 4, 1991: The Walkers; Dutch Treat II; Acid Rain; A Few Minutes with Andy Rooney (XXIII: 47) Program # 2347

August 11, 1991: Saddam's Billions; Brucification; Harry Reasoner (XXIII: 48) Program # 2348

August 18, 1991: All in the Family; Keep Your Mouth Shut; 10 Extraordinary Women (XXIII: 49) Program # 2349

August 25, 1991: What Now?; The Numbers Game; A Question of Mercy (XXIII: 50) Program # 2350

September 1, 1991: Project 2000; Jack Lemmon; War Games; A Few Minutes with Andy Rooney (XXIII: 51) Program # 2351

September 8, 1991: Room 19; Cream Puff; A Letter from Jermarr; A Few Minutes with Andy Rooney (XXIII: 52) Program # 2352

September 15, 1991: Made in China; Epidemic; Live or Die?; A Few Minutes with Andy Rooney (XXIV: 1) Program # 2353

September 22, 1991: The Secret Life of Dennis Levine; Thoral Sundt, M.D.; The Last Sioux Brave; A Few Minutes with Andy Rooney (XXIV: 2) Program # 2354

September 29, 1991: The Trials of Juanita; The KGB; 1–800–CON MAN; A Few Minutes with Andy Rooney (XXIV: 3) Program # 2355

October 4, 1991: Special Edition: The Entertainers (XXIV: 4) Program # 60-MSP-1

October 20, 1991: The "Trashing" of Clayton Hartwig; The Poison Umbrella; A Few Minutes with Andy Rooney (XXIV: 5) Program # 60-MSP-2

October 27, 1991: What About Prozac?; Texas Rules; "Welfare for the Wealthy"; A Few Minutes with Andy Rooney (XXIV: 6) Program #60-MSP-3

November 3, 1991: No MSG; Plugging the Leaks; George Bush vs. George Bush; A Few Minutes with Any Rooney (XXIV: 7) Program # 60-MSP-4

November 10, 1991: Friendly Fire; Norplant; Easy Money in Hard Times; A Few Minutes with Andy Rooney (XXIV: 8) Program # 60-MSP-5

November 17, 1991: Saddam's Secrets; The French Paradox; The Psycho Squad; A Few Minutes with Andy Rooney (XXIV: 9) Program # 60-MSP-6

November 24, 1991: The Teamsters; Barbra; Just Another Killing?; A Few Minutes with Andy Rooney (XXIV: 10) Program # 60-MSP-7

December 1, 1991: Smoking to Live; Camille; Getting Away with Murder; A Few Minutes with Andy Rooney (XXIV: 11) Program # 60-MSP-8

December 8, 1991: Mississippi Christmas Tree; Sound of Music; Fur or Against?; A Few Minutes with Andy Rooney (XXIV: 12) Program # 60-MSP-9

December 15, 1991: Halcion; The Great Dane; Take the Money and Run (XXIV: 13) Program # 60-MSP-10

December 22, 1991: Hussein & Hussein; Eric Ramsey of Auburn; Jessye; A Few Minutes with Andy Rooney (XXIV: 14) Program # 60-MSP-11

December 29, 1991: Georgia; Mea; Rikers Island; A Few Minutes with Andy Rooney (XXIV: 15) Program # 60-MSP-12

"60 MINUTES" 1992 PROGRAMS

January 5, 1992: Time Bombs; Murder She Writes; Children of the Berlin Wall; A Few Minutes with Andy Rooney (XXIV: 16) Program # 60-MSP-13

January 12, 1992: Black Market Babies; Don't Leave Home; Colin Powell; A Few Minutes with Andy Rooney (XXIV: 17) Program # 60-MSP-14

January 19, 1992: World's Biggest Shopping Spree; Nayirah; Charlotte Austin; A Few Minutes with Andy Rooney (XXIV: 18) Program # 60-MSP-15

February 9, 1992: Bang, Bang, You're Dead; Buy American; Mirror, Mirror on the Wall; A Few Minutes with Andy Rooney (XXIV: 21) Program # 60-MSP-16)

February 16, 1992: The Sting; Damn Yankees; Car Seats; A Few Minutes with Andy Rooney (XXIV: 22) Program # 60-MSP-17

February 23, 1992: Saddam's Killing Fields; Life, Death, and Politics; Malcolm X; A Few Minutes with Andy Rooney (XXIV: 23) Program # 60-MSP-18

March 1, 1992: Red Cell; Dr. Mengele's Laboratory; The Oregon Plan; A Few Minutes with Andy Rooney (XXIV: 24) Program # 60-MSP-19 (Anita Darnes Audio/Video Transcript)

March 8, 1992: Another Karen Silkwood?; Neil Simon; American Gothic Gone Mad; A Few Minutes with Andy Rooney (XXIV: 25) Program # 60-MSP-20 (Anita Darnes Audio/Video Transcript)

March 15, 1992: Bill and Kathy Swan; Heeere's Jay Leno!; Yusef Salaam; A Few Minutes with Andy Rooney (XXIV: 26) Program # 60-MSP-21

March 22, 1992: Emily's List; Mob Girl; Leonardo Mercado Is Dead; A Few Minutes with Andy Rooney (XXIV: 27) Program # 60-MSP-22

March 29, 1992: Kissinger; Spielberg; H. Ross Perot; A Few Minutes with Andy Rooney (XXIV: 28) Program # 60-MSP-23

"60 MINUTES" 1993 PROGRAM

November 14, 1993: "60 Minutes" 25th Anniversary (XXVI: 9) Retrospective Program from 1968 to 1993 (Livingston, N.J.: Burrelle's Information Services, 1993)

Appendix II

"48 Hours" Broadcasts

March 4, 1992: Stalker; Fatal Obsession; Fan Mail; Stranger; House Calls; Starry Eyes; Fatal Obsession (Number 187)

March 11, 1992: Manhunt; Predator: Born to Be Wild; Robodeer; They're Back; Wild at Heart (Number 188)

March 18, 1992: Hanging Tough; American Nightmare; Close to Home (Part One); Chain Reaction; Dream Girl; Hard Lesson; Close to Home (Part Two); Starting Over (Number 189)

March 25, 1992: Who Killed These Girls?; The Murders; Homicide Squad; Country Girls; Missing; Afraid; Suspects; Homicide Squad; We Will Not Forget (Number 190)

April 1, 1992: Treasure Hunt; Gold Coast; Found and Lost; Child's Play; X Marks the Spot; Underworld; Bonfire of the Manatees; Bottom Line; Taking the Plunge (Number 191)

April 8, 1992: Murder or Madness; Rampage; Matter of Opinion; Cry for Help; Case History; Once a Killer; Back on Track; Judgment Day; Next Week (Number 192)

April 15, 1992: Family Secret; The Arrangement; The Search; The Visitor; Lost and Found; The Choice: Lost and Found (Day Two); Giving Up Baby; Next Week (Number 193)

April 22, 1992: The Heroin Connection; Hide and Seek; Raw Recruits; Sidewalk Sale; Consumer Reports; Opium Country; War Story; Dead End; Next Week (Number 194)

May 6, 1992: Scam; Dialing for Dollars; The Pigeon; Fast Buck; Lucky Day; It's a Steal; Family Business; The Player; Next Week (Number 195)

May 13, 1992: Baby Hope; Mystery on the Menu (Part One); Scene of the
    Crime; Expert Witness; Dead Reckoning; Mystery on the Menu
    (Part Two); Rare Medium; Hearing Is Believing; Burning Questions;
    Grave Doubts; Expert Witness; Mystery on the Menu (Part Three);
    Next Week (Number 196) (Two-hour special)

May 20, 1992: Pet Passion; Love Story; Homeless; My Best Friend; Can We
    Talk?; Cat Call; Homeless; House Calls; Party Animals; Next Week
    (Number 197)

May 27, 1992: The Killer Next Door; 'Til Death Do Us Part; Learn and
    Live; Need to Know; Bombshell; Calculated Risk; Buying Time;
    Fatal Legacy; Next Week (Number 198)

January 13, 1993: Two hour special interview with President-elect Bill
    Clinton, conducted by Dan Rather (Anita Darnes Audio/Video
    Transcript)

"Street Stories" Broadcasts

November 5, 1992: Introduction; Critical Condition; Family Ties; Current News: Oregon Measure 9 Protest (anti-homosexuality measure defeated); Jim Sharp HIV Infection; Arson in Lawrence, Massachusetts (Livingston, N.J.: Burrelle's Transcripts, 1992, no volume or number indicated)

November 12, 1992: Introduction; Killing Time (Malmedy massacre in World War II); Wiped Out (Bob Kearns, inventor of intermittent windshield wiper); Bad Blood (crime family member stricken with AIDS); Home on the Range (ranches and real estate)

November 19, 1992: Introduction; Highway Robbers (carjacking in Detroit); Trade Secrets (American and Russian former spies meet); Accident-Prone (Roberta Baskin investigation into cases from National Highway Traffic Safety Administration files); Son of a Gun (circus cannon performers)

December 10, 1992: Introduction; Restoring Hope (Operation for Peacekeeping in Somalia); Mother's Intuition (breast implant patient); Sir Mix-a-Lot (musician); Detective Story (private eyes)

December 12, 1992: Introduction; Tyler, Texas (drug-racial incident); Dental Hygiene (Part I) (dangers of AIDS from dental implements); Dental Hygiene (Part II); New World (Harry Smith visits new immigrants in New York)

December 17, 1992: Introduction; Blood Feud (hemophiliacs with AIDS); Knowing the Score (Croatian artist and protest songs); Broken Homes (assistance to Florida hurricane victims); Street Stories 1992 (montage with Clintons; Bush; space shuttle launch; view of earth;

Kristi Yamaguchi; Reginald Denny beating; Las Vegas attack on Reagan; Bush on Somalia; Amsterdam plane crash; Martha Teichner from South Africa; Woody Allen; Mike Tyson; Bush in Japan; Pope John Paul II; Boris Yeltsin; Elvis stamp; earthquake damage; Diana and Charles; fire; Johnny Carson farewell; tall ship; Bush; Pat Buchanan; Governor Clinton; Ross Perot; Tsongas campaign; Ross Perot; Jerry Brown; Bob Kerrey; Tom Harkin; Bill Clinton; Bush; Perot; Bush; Clinton; Bush; Clinton; Dan Quayle; Al Gore; Tsongas; pH Factor; Clinton acceptance; Bush acceptance; Quayle; Clinton with saxophone; Perot listening; George and Barbara Bush; Al Gore; Admiral Stockdale; Perot; Jerry Brown; Clinton; Perot; "Murphy Brown"; Quayle; Bush; Clinton; Perot; Dan Rather on election night; Sarajevo scenes; Yo-Yo-Ma performing; Sarajevo correspondent; Teichner from Bosnia; Olympic footage; David Benoit performance; Olympics; Bonnie Blair; Magic Johnson; Hurricane Andrew damage; Mary Chapin-Carpenter; LA police officers' trial; LA riots; Rodney King; LA riots coverage; footage of LA and children from around the world

January 7, 1993: Germ Warfare Part One (Deborah Norville's first story as correspondent on tuberculosis revival); Germ Warfare Part Two (efforts at government control); Talk of the Town (TB with shipyard workers in Maine); Marion Barry's campaign for DC city council and oath-taking as Ward 8 Councilman; follow-up on Gregory Scarpa; Buddhist priest murder in Arizona

February 25, 1993: Introduction; Cat and Mouse (detective and suspect); Forging a Friendship (tabloid lonely hearts ad); Off the Books (underground economy and "nanny" tax); The Boy Next Door (Clark Gable's hometown, Cadiz, Ohio)

March 4, 1992: Introduction; Not in My Neighborhood (child molester cases); Overdrive (truckers' accidents); Murder or Mercy (Dr. Jack Kevorkian's brushes with Michigan law); Skin Deep (Michael Jackson's illness with vitiligo)

March 11, 1993: Introduction; Lone Star Scandal (Branch Davidian cult and brushes with law); Second Thoughts (Dr. Beverly McMillan, legal abortion provider in Mississippi); How Much Hope (Odone family featured in *Lorenzo's Oil* film); Being There (David Koresh compound near Waco)

April 1, 1993: Introduction; Porn in the 'Hood (censorship and porno raids in suburban streets in Forest Hills, Long Island); Fatal Practice (murder of Dr. David Gunn in Florida abortion controversy); Plan of Attack (slaying of ATF agents in Texas); No Identifiable Reason (little girl's medical mystery)

April 8, 1993: Children as Innocent Prey (Oregon anti-stalking law); Drawing the Line (fear in Koreatown after LA riots); Lights! Cameras! Taxes! (IRS crackdown on Hollywood extravagance); Update on Mississippi jail fraud

Appendix IV

"20/20" and "PrimeTime Live" Broadcasts

"20/20" BROADCASTS

March 15, 1991: General Norman Schwarzkopf I (Barbara Walters)

May 24, 1991: Abortion Doctor (Lynn Sherr); Ivana Trump; Gulf War Heroes

September 20, 1991: Pension Swindles (Lynn Sherr); Money Magazine Survey (Hugh Downs)

March 13, 1992: Joan Lunden Alimony Dispute (Barbara Walters)

March 27, 1992: Leona Helmsley (Barbara Walters); Wrongly Convicted Inmate/Lester Jeeter

April 3, 1992: Kennedy Assassination; Green Card Immigrants

April 10, 1992: Arthur Ashe; The Victim Within/CIA; The Toughest Prison/Marion, Illinois, Reformatory; Moles That Weren't Moles/ James Jesus Angleton

May 29, 1992: H. Ross Perot I (Barbara Walters); Single-Sex Schools (John Stossel)

August 21, 1992: General Norman Schwarzkopf II (Barbara Walters); Courtroom Security; Auto Pollution Control; Florida Religious Sect

August 28, 1992: Friendly Fire; Whistle-blowers and Corporate Cover-ups; Children in the Same Bed

September 4, 1992: Trial of Texas Minister (Hugh Downs)

September 11, 1992: Boat People's Reunion in Vietnam (Tom Jarriell); The Hidden Scandal (Hugh Downs, Barbara Walters)

September 25, 1992: General Norman Schwarzkopf III (Barbara Walters); Governor Bill Clinton; Gregory Kay (Suit Against Mother)

October 2, 1992: H. Ross Perot II (Barbara Walters)
November 20, 1992: The Skin Game; The Man Behind the Badge/Daily life
     of police officers; Centenarians
December 4, 1992: John Lennon's Killer at Attica (Barbara Walters);
     Florida Victims of Hurricane Andrew
December 11, 1992: Federal Gun Laws; Heart Arrythmia (Hugh Downs,
     Barbara Walters); Jerry Lewis
December 25, 1992: British War Brides; Scam (Hugh Downs)

"PRIMETIME LIVE" BROADCASTS

February 7, 1991: General Norman Schwarzkopf (Diane Sawyer)
August 28, 1991: Inside the Kremlin (Diane Sawyer); Boris Yeltsin
     (Diane Sawyer with Sam Donaldson)
September 19, 1991: Hafez Assad of Syria (Diane Sawyer)
November 14, 1991: Whistle-blower; Magic Johnson
August 13, 1992: Bosnian Civil War I, II, III, IV
October 8, 1992: Bryan's Murder in New York; Madonna; Presidential
     Debates (Diane Sawyer, Sam Donaldson)
November 24, 1992: Jerry Lewis

Appendix V

"Dateline NBC" Broadcasts

September 8, 1992: Child Abduction by Spouse (Stone Phillips); Hillary
    Clinton (Jane Pauley)
September 15, 1992: Neil Bush Scandal (Pauley/Phillips)
November 11, 1992: Passionate Sex in Marriage
December 1, 1992: Homeopathy; Bank Robberies; "Real World Make
    Believe" (Pauley/Phillips)
December 15, 1992: Rapists and Parole; Kidnap Victim's Mother (Pauley/
    Phillips)

Bibliography

Abramson, Jeffrey B., P. Christopher Arterton, and Garry R. Orren. *The Electronic Commonwealth*. New York: Basic Books, 1988.

Adams, William C., ed. *Television Coverage of International Affairs*. Norwood, NJ: Ablex Publishing Corp., 1982.

"Ahoy, Cable Pirates: Pay Up or Ship Out." *TV Guide* 40, no. 34 (August 15–21, 1992): 20.

"All-Time Best: News Show Magazine: 60 Minutes." *TV Guide* 41, no. 16 (April 17–23, 1993): 69.

Alter, Jonathan. "Between the Lines: It Isn't All Junk Food: Believe It or Not, Prime-Time TV News Is More Informative Than Ever Before." *Newsweek* CXXIII, no. 15 (April 11, 1994): 66.

Alterman, Eric. "Moyers on Washington." *Washington Post Magazine* (September 1, 1991): 22–23.

Arnett, Peter. *Live from the Battlefield*. New York: Simon and Schuster Audioworks, 1994.

Auletta, Ken. *Three Blind Mice: How the TV Networks Lost Their Way*. New York: Random House, 1991.

"The Best and Worst According to Nielsen." *TV Guide* 41, no. 22 (May 29–June 4, 1993): 16–17.

"The Best: Newsperson." *TV Guide* 41, no. 16 (April 17–23, 1993): 70–71.

"The Best: News Shows/Magazines." *TV Guide* 41, no. 16 (April 17–23, 1993): 8–12.

The Best of 60 Minutes, Vol. 1. CBS/Fox Video, 1984.

The Best of 60 Minutes, Vol. 2. CBS/Fox Video, 1985.

Boyer, Peter J. *Who Killed CBS? The Undoing of America's Number One News Network*. New York: Random House, 1988.

Brodsky, Art. "Capitolism: Broadcast Views, The Word of FCC Overseer Milt

Gross Carries the Word of Law." *City Paper* (Washington), (October 26, 1990): 12.

Bundy, McGeorge. *Danger and Survival: Choices About the Bomb in the First 50 Years.* New York: Random House, 1988.

Burns, Ken. *Empire of the Air: The Men Who Made Radio.* PBS Home Video. Los Angeles: Radio Pioneers Film Project, 1991.

Cablevision Magazine (August 30, 1982): 18.

CBS News. *60 Minutes Verbatim: Who Said What to Whom: The Complete Text of 114 Stories with Mike Wallace, Morley Safer, Dan Rather, Harry Reasoner.* New York: Arno Press/CBS News, 1980.

———. *"60 Minutes" Segment, "An American Family,"* July 15, 1990. Ambrose Video Publishing, Inc.

———. *"60 Minutes" Segment, "The House on Barlow Street,"* July 15, 1990. Ambrose Video Publishing, Inc.

———. "60 Minutes." Transcript (XXVI: 9), November 14, 1993, p. 2.

Chambers, Whittaker. *Witness.* New York: Doubleday, 1959.

"Cheers 'n' Jeers: ABC, CBS and NBC Have Devoted More Time to Policy Issues, Deserve Cheers for 1992 Coverage." *TV Guide* 40, no. 40 (October 3–9, 1992): 6.

"Cheers 'n' Jeers: Cheers to '60 Minutes.' " *TV Guide* 40, no. 50 (December 12–18, 1992): 6.

Cronkite, Walter, Narrator. *Remembering* LIFE: *An American Experience.* Beverly Hills, CA: Active Home Video, 1985.

Davis, Jeff. "The Couch Critic: Day One." *TV Guide* 41, no. 17 (April 24–30, 1993): 18.

Denton, Robert E., Jr., ed. *The Media and the Persian Gulf War.* Westport, CT: Praeger, 1993.

Diamond, Edwin. *The Media Show: The Changing Face of the News, 1985–1990.* Cambridge: MIT Press, 1991.

Douglas, Susan J. *Inventing American Broadcasting.* Baltimore: The Johns Hopkins University Press, 1987.

Dreifus, Claudia. "The Midlife Triumphs of Cokie Roberts." *TV Guide* 41, no. 25 (June 19–25, 1993): 22–26.

Eisenhower, Dwight D. *The Eisenhower Diaries.* Edited by Robert H. Ferrell. New York: W. W. Norton & Co., 1981.

Ellerbee, Linda. ". . . And I Lived." *TV Guide* 41, no. 16 (April 17–23, 1993): 13–17.

Elm, Joanna. "Jane Pauley: My Life After Today." *TV Guide* 38, no. 11 (March 10, 1990): 28–29.

Else, John. *The Day After Trinity.* Video documentary. Pyramid Home Video, 1981.

Fat Man and Little Boy: The Story of the Extraordinary People Who Changed Our World. Paramount Pictures, 1989.

Foote, Joe S. *Television Access and Political Power: The Networks, the Presidency, and the "Loyal Opposition."* New York: Praeger, 1990.

Frank, Reuven. *Out of Thin Air: The Brief Wonderful Life of Network News.* New York: Simon & Schuster, 1991.

Freeman, Mike. "The Economics of First-Run Reality: Growth of News Magazines Has Been Somewhat Arrested by Cop and Rescue Series; Weeklies Form

Strategic Partnerships, Target Specialized Demographics." *Broadcasting & Cable* (April 12, 1993): 34–37

———. "Fox's 'Front Page.' " *Broadcasting & Cable* (June 28, 1993): 17.

Friendly, Fred W. *Due to Circumstances Beyond Our Control*. New York: Vintage Books, 1968.

Gannett Foundation Media Center. *The Media at War: The Press and the Persian Gulf Conflict*. New York: Gannett Foundation/Freedom Forum, 1991.

Gelman, Morrie. "Madison Avenue Predicts Prime Time." *Broadcasting & Cable* (July 19, 1993): 18–20.

Gerard, Jeremy. "Prime Time Comes Alive: By Shaking Up Her Image, Diane Sawyer Revives Her Career—and Her Show." *TV Guide* 40, no. 47 (November 21–27, 1992): 8–13.

Goldberg, Robert, and Gerald Jay Goldberg. *Anchors: Brokaw, Jennings, Rather and the Evening News*. New York: Birch Lane Press/Carol Publishing Group, 1990.

Golson, Barry, and Peter Ross Range. "Wotta Year! The TV Campaign That Transformed American Politics—George Bush Called It 'Wacky,' Bill Clinton, a 'Revolution.' " *TV Guide* 40, no. 45 (November 7–13, 1992): 16–21.

Goodnight and Good Luck: Edward R. Murrow Television Collection. Vol. 1, CBS News/Fox Video, 1993.

Goodnight and Good Luck: Vol. 2, The Best of See It Now. CBS News/Fox Video, 1993.

"Grapevine: Convention Wisdom: As the Republicans Prepare for a Grand Old Party in Houston, We Take a Look at TV's Part in the Proceedings." *TV Guide* 40, no. 33 (August 15–21, 1992): 4, 5.

"Grapevine: What I Watch—Peggy Noonan." *TV Guide* 40, no. 34 (August 22–28, 1992): 28.

"Grapevine Sound Bite: 'Bill Clinton's Brother Sings. Tipper Gore Plays the Drums. Clinton Plays the Sax. This Isn't the Democratic Party—This is the Partridge Family.'—Jay Leno." *TV Guide* 40, no. 40 (October 3–9, 1992): 4.

Halberstam, David. *The Best and the Brightest*. Greenwich, CT: Fawcett Crest Books, 1972.

———. *The Powers That Be*. New York: Random House, 1978.

Hiss, Alger. *In the Court of Public Opinion*. New York: Scribners, 1961.

James, Clive. "TV and the Fame Game: Who's a Celebrity—and Why—in the Age of Worldwide TV? A British Journalist, Host of a New Eight-Hour PBS Documentary, Tells What It Takes." *TV Guide* 41, no. 23 (June 5–11, 1993): 24–27.

Jennings, Peter. *45/85: America and the World Since World War II. Vol. 2*. ABC News Video, 1985.

Jones, Dylan. "Top Ratings Return with Rooney." *USA Today* (March 6, 1990): 3D.

Kellner, Douglas. *Television and the Crisis of Democracy*. Boulder, CO: Westview Press, 1990.

Kendrick, Alexander. *Prime Time: The Life of Edward R. Murrow*. New York: Avon Books, 1969.

Kerbel, Matthew Robert. *Edited for Television: CNN, ABC and the 1992 Presidential Campaign*. Boulder, CO: Westview Press, 1994.

Kessler, Judy. "Exclusive Excerpt: 'Gumbelgate'—How Bryant's Famous Memo and Jane Pauley's Departure Almost Torpedoed 'Today.' " *TV Guide* 40, no. 40 (October 3–9, 1992): 18–21.

"Kroft, Vieira: Up to the 'Minutes.' " *USA Today* (March 6, 1990): 3D.

Kumar, Martha Joynt. *Wired for Sound and Pictures: The President and White House Communications Policies.* Baltimore: Johns Hopkins University Press, Forthcoming.

Kunetza, James W. *Oppenheimer: The Years of Risk.* Englewood Cliffs, NJ: Prentice-Hall, 1982.

Lee, Martin A., and Norton Solomon. *Unreliable Sources: A Guide to Detecting Bias in News Media.* New York: Lyle Stuart/Carol Publishing Group, 1991.

Lichter, S. Robert, Stanley Rothman, and Linda S. Lichter. *The Media Elite.* Bethesda, MD: Adler and Adler, 1986.

Lieberman, David. "Too Much of a Good Thing: An Embarrassing Blunder at One Newsmagazine May Be a Symptom of Broadcast Journalism Running Amok." *TV Guide* 41, no. 10 (March 6–12, 1993): 24–26.

———. "TV Guide Update: NBC—the Dateline Aftermath: Now the Good News—Maybe?" *TV Guide* 41, no. 11 (March 13–19, 1993): 33.

Logan, Michael. "A New 'Page' in News: A Newsmag Aims for the Young and Shoots from the Hip." *TV Guide* 41, no. 26 (June 26–July 2, 1993): 28–29.

MacArthur, John R. *Second Front: Censorship and Propaganda in the Gulf War.* New York: Hill and Wang, 1992.

McClellan, Steve. "Judge Rules CBS Can Be Sued over 'Street' Story." *Broadcasting & Cable* (July 5, 1993): 14–15.

———. "March 7 Is 'Day One' for ABC: New Show Is First of Several." *Broadcasting & Cable* (March 1, 1993): 12, 13.

Marin, Rick. "Make Room for Connie." *TV Guide* 41, no. 23 (June 5–11, 1993): 8–14.

Mitgang, Herbert. *Dangerous Dossiers: Exposing the Secret War Against America's Greatest Authors.* New York: Donald I. Fine, 1988.

Murrow, Edward R. *Automation.* CBS, Video Yesteryear, No. 241, airdate June 9, 1957.

———. *Harvest of Shame.* CBS Reports. Narrated by Dan Rather. Fox Video Set, 1993.

Museum of Broadcasting. *Walter Cronkite: Rare Voices of the 20th Century.* Museum of Broadcasting audiotape, side two, band five. New York: Museum of Broadcasting, 1981.

Nimmo, Dan, and James E. Combs. *Mediated Political Realities.* 2nd ed. New York: Longman, 1988.

"Off the Air: NBC News President, Burned by Staged Fire and GM, Will Resign." *Wall Street Journal* CCXXI, no. 41 (March 2, 1993): A1, A12.

Ogden, Christopher. *Life of the Party: The Biography of Pamela Digby Churchill Hayward Harriman.* Boston: Little, Brown & Co., 1984.

Oppenheimer, Jerry. *Barbara Walters: An Unauthorized Biography.* New York: St. Martin's Press, 1990.

Paper, Lewis J. *Empire: William S. Paley and the Making of CBS.* New York: St. Martin's Press, 1987.

Park, Bert E., M.D. *Ailing, Aging, Addicted: Studies of Compromised Leadership.* Lexington: University Press of Kentucky, 1992.

Persico, Joseph E. *Edward R. Murrow: An American Original*. New York: Dell Publishing, 1988.

Person to Person with Edward R. Murrow. Video Yesteryear, 1981.

Pfau, Richard. *No Sacrifice Too Great: The Life of Lewis L. Strauss*. Charlottesville: University Press of Virginia, 1984.

Polskin, Howard. "CBS Fired Him, Promoted Her. That Makes 60 Minutes' Meredith Vieira and Her Husband . . . Strange Bedfellows." *TV Guide* 38, no. 13 (March 31, 1990): 17–19.

Porter, William E. *Assault on the Media: The Nixon Years*. Ann Arbor: University of Michigan Press, 1977.

Press, Charles, and Kenneth VerBurg. *American Politics and Journalists*. Glenview, IL: Scott, Foresman, 1991.

"Prime Time: Chung May Gun for News-Mag Gig." *TV Guide* 40, no. 33 (August 15–21, 1992): 25.

"Prime Time Predictions for 1993–94." *Broadcasting & Cable* (July 19, 1993): 22.

"Pro and Retrospective." *Broadcasting* (December 17, 1990): 8.

Rabi, I. I., et al. *Oppenheimer: The Story of One of the Most Remarkable Personalities of the 20th Century*. New York: Charles Scribner's Sons, 1969.

Range, Peter Ross. "Politics: Clintonites Miffed as Two Networks Boycott Press Meet." *TV Guide* 41, no. 27 (July 3–9, 1993): 34.

Rather, Dan. *I Remember*. New York: Simon & Schuster, 1991.

Rather, Dan, with Mickey Herskowitz. *The Camera Never Blinks Twice: The Further Adventures of a Television Journalist*. New York: William Morrow, 1994.

Reasoner, Harry. *Before the Colors Fade*. Boston: Little, Brown, 1981.

"Reasoner's New Role." *USA Today* (March 6, 1990): 1D.

Reibstein, Larry. "The Battle of the TV News Magazine Shows: Trash + Class = Cash." *Newsweek* CXXIII, no. 15 (April 11, 1994): 61–65.

Rudolph, Ileane. "See Jane Run: Pauley Puts a Personal Stamp on Her Weekly Show." *TV Guide* 39, no. 1 (January 5, 1991): 8–11.

———. "Soft News Is in Vogue at Today." *TV Guide* 41, no. 23 (June 5–11, 1993): 38.

Sabato, Larry J. *Feeding Frenzy: How Attack Journalism Has Transformed American Politics*. New York: Free Press, 1991.

Safer, Morley. *Flashbacks: On Returning to Vietnam*. New York: Random House, 1990.

Salant, Richard. *CBS News Standards*. New York: CBS News.

———. *See It Now, Starring Edward R. Murrow: The Hydrogen Bomb*. Golden TV Classics, 1986.

Sevareid, Eric. *Not So Wild a Dream*. New York: Random House, 1961.

Shales, Tom. "TV Column." *Washington Post* (December 10, 1990): C1, C3.

Shirer, William L. *20th Century Journey: The Nightmare Years, 1930–1940*. Boston: Little, Brown, 1984.

———. *20th Century Journey: A Native's Return, 1945–1948*. Boston: Little, Brown, 1990.

"The 60 Minutes Team Tells: The Toughest Stories We've Ever Tackled." *TV Guide* 39, no. 3 (January 19–25, 1991): 2–6.

Slater, Robert. *This . . . Is CBS: A Chronicle of 60 Years*. Englewood Cliffs, NJ: Prentice-Hall, 1988.

Smith, Conrad. *Media and Apocalypse: News Coverage of the Yellowstone Forest*

Fires, Exxon Valdez Oil Spill, and Loma Prieta Earthquake. Westport, CT: Greenwood Press, 1992.

Smith, Craig Allen, and Kathy B. Smith. *The White House Speaks: Presidential Leadership as Persuasion.* Westport, CT: Praeger, 1994.

Smoller, Frederic T. *The Six O'Clock Presidency: A Theory of Presidential Press Relations in the Age of Television.* Westport, CT: Praeger, 1990.

Span, Paula. "Tribute to the Titan of CBS." *Washington Post* (November 13, 1990): C1, C3.

Spragens, William C. *The Presidency and the Mass Media in the Age of Television.* Lanham, MD: University Press of America, 1978.

———. *From Spokesman to Press Secretary: White House Media Operations.* Lanham, MD: University Press of America, 1980.

———. "Security Clearances in the Eisenhower Era: The Case of Dr. J. Robert Oppenheimer." Paper presented at Eisenhower Centennial Symposium, Gettysburg (PA) College, October 1990.

Stein, Harry. "Our Times/By Harry Stein: Watch Out! That Just Might Be a Bimbo Eruption Over There." *TV Guide* 40, no. 34 (August 22–28, 1992): 29.

———. "TV Update: Our Times, a Column About Values and TV—a Firebrand with a Showboating Style Easily Steals the Show." *TV Guide* 40, no. 49 (December 5–11, 1992): 41.

———. "TV Update: Our Times, a Column About Values and TV." *TV Guide* 40, no. 50 (December 12–18, 1992): 33.

———. "TV Update: Our Times, a Column About Values and TV, 'How TV Triumphs—and Trips up—in Somalia.' " *TV Guide* 41, no. 3 (January 16–22, 1993): 43.

———. "TV Update: Our Times: Today's News Shows Treat Us As Though We're Stupid." *TV Guide* 41, no. 11 (March 13–19, 1993): 35.

Stern, Philip M., et al. *The Oppenheimer Case: Security on Trial.* New York: Harper & Row, 1969.

Stouffer, Samuel, et al. "Communism, Conformity and Civil Rights." *Public Administration Review* 16 (Winter 1956): 40–52.

"Summer's Top 10s." *TV Guide* 41, no. 24 (June 12–18, 1993): 8–19.

"Tartikoff's Tricks of the Trade: TV's Programming Champ Lists a Few Lessons from His Glory Days at NBC." *TV Guide* 40, no. 42 (October 17–23, 1992): 15–17.

Thomas, Jackie. "TV Guide's Top 20 Report Card." *TV Guide* 41, no. 6 (February 6–12, 1993): 24–32.

"TV Guide Update: CBS Has Stars in Its Eyes as It Pairs Dan and Connie." *TV Guide* 41, no. 22 (May 29–June 4, 1993): 41.

"TV Update: The Politics of Hollywood," *TV Guide* 40, no. 34 (August 22–28, 1992): 28.

"TV Update: Pundits Ponder: Do Those Debates Matter After All?" *TV Guide* 40, no. 42 (October 17–23, 1992): 41–42.

"TV Update: Reaction—NBC News Responds to 'Gumbelgate.' " *TV Guide* 40, no. 40 (October 3–9, 1992): 31.

Wallace, Mike, and Gary Paul Gates. *Close Encounters: Mike Wallace's Own Story.* New York: William Morrow, 1984.

Wanniski, Jude. *Repap 1992 Media Guide: A Critical Review of the Media.* Morristown, NJ: Polyconomics, 1992.

Washburn, Philo C. *Broadcasting Propaganda: International Radio Broadcasting and the Construction of Political Reality*. Westport, CT: Praeger, 1992.

Whicker, Marcia, James Pfiffner, and Raymond Moore. *The Presidency and the Persian Gulf War*. Westport, CT: Praeger, 1993.

Whittemore, Hank. *CNN The Inside Story: How a Band of Mavericks Changed the Face of Television News*. Boston: Little, Brown & Co., 1990.

Williams, Huntington. *Beyond Control: ABC and the Fate of the Networks*. New York: Atheneum, 1989.

"Will Republican Convention Coverage Bash Bush?" *TV Guide* 40, no. 33 (August 15–21, 1992): 25.

Winfield, Betty Houchin. *FDR and the News Media*. New York: Columbia University Press, 1985.

Index

About the Author

WILLIAM C. SPRAGENS is professor emeritus at Bowling Green State University in Ohio. He is also the owner of Spragens Research/Analysis, a consulting firm in Herndon, Virginia.

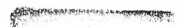